The
Appetite
CONNECTION:

Six Steps to
Your Delicious Life
and the Body You
Long For

Dr. Denise Lamothe

"*The Appetite Connection* is a delight and must-read for anyone struggling with emotional overeating or stress eating. Dr. Denise has compiled the best of the best advice and ideas on taking control of your Appetite and your life. Each chapter is sprinkled with gold nuggets of not only the latest information on the subject, but action steps that will deliver dramatic results. Speaking from personal experience, she delivers a message that guides the reader to find customized and holistic solutions that lead to vibrant health and wellness. The numerous suggestions ensure that the reader has a wealth of options to choose from in crafting an individual strategy to gain balance, radiant health, and a positive "can do" attitude. Read *The Appetite Connection* before you take another bite!"

—Peter Martino, retired colonel, U.S. Marine Corps Reserve

"This empowering book will inspire, teach you to accept yourself, and assist you in gaining a holistic view of eating. Dr. Lamothe is an engaging author who has incorporated real-life examples that are easy to identify with and allows the reader to regain control of her eating and begin to live the life she has always wanted to live, in health and happiness. Through this book you will make peace with food and your body."

—Mimi L. Sorg, LCSW, CPC

"Dr. Lamothe has created an outstanding sequel to her first book, *The Taming of the Chew*. In *The Appetite Connection* she offers practical suggestions for gaining control of one's Appetite, making self-loving choices, and maintaining balance of one's body, mind, and spirit. This book is of great value to anyone struggling with eating issues, and I will be recommending it to many of the clients I treat."

—Wayne Kieran Cunningham, PhD, LADC, LCMHC

"Clear, concise, an easy read for all of us with eating issues. This is not a book about dieting! This is a book about our total well-being. Dr. Lamothe gives us an understanding of how and why we use food to cope with issues in our lives and at the same time teaches us how to enjoy life while getting control over food. Most of all, this is an entertaining, fun, insightful, and refreshing read, filled with inspiring stories of real people who have transformed their lives by following Dr. Denise's guidance, by getting off the dieting roller coaster and shedding those pounds forever."

—Elaine Schubert, BS, MS, health and physical education teacher, athletic coach, and group leader of an international weight-loss program

"Dr. Denise Lamothe gets it. Not only has she been there, she provides concrete examples, exercises, and strategies to get you to look at yourself and dive deeper into your emotional eating past, present, and future. I wish I had had this resource when I was not only losing my weight, but during my fourteen years of working with people who were engaged in the weight-loss battle. Her ideas, research, and knowledge will definitely help you to understand that why you eat is equally if not more important than what you eat. Let Dr. Denise help you find out what's eating you!"

—Rich DiGirolamo, professional speaker, counselor, and fourteen-year guide to thousands of people for an international weight-loss organization

"Beyond cabbage soup diets, healthy eating plans, life coaches, fat acceptance, and everything else comes this new book, *The Appetite Connection*. I have renewed hope. I am no longer afraid. Many times I'd heard how we eat to cover our feelings, and I agreed. But the sneaky ways I sabotaged myself kept me in the cycle of self-destructive behavior. I knew this, but I just couldn't see how I was doing it. Now, I can and I'm touching hope again. Dr. Denise exposes the root causes of this complex issue and offers tools to help us heal—tools that actually work!"

—Sheri Donica, radio host of
The Skinny on Fat Show, Real Coaching Radio

"There are many books about weight loss currently riding the shelves, many authored by highly educated and accredited experts. They are not all penned by people who 'lived' the journey. Dr. Denise's heart comes through in every chapter, and her soul is laid bare inside each case study. She is here today because she was THERE, where you may be right now. She walks her talk and has left big footprints for you to follow. Choose her path...choose life!"

—Steve Gamlin, professional speaker, "Inspired By Steve," author
of *20 To Life: In a Good Way* and *Oh Yeah! (Another Quote Book)*

"Dr. Denise is a very wise woman. Her gentle, simple, and powerful suggestions will help you become the person you are meant to be."

—Debby Hoffman Adair, author of *Find Something
Nice to Say: The Power of Compliments*

"*The Appetite Connection* is packed with information yet is an easy read. I found it informative and appreciated that I never felt I was reading a textbook. Dr. Denise has crafted an amazing book that would be helpful for anyone struggling with any form of addiction."

—Maralyn Morrissey, former manager of a
halfway house for recovering alcoholics

Published by Questover Books

PO Box 1013
Exeter, New Hampshire 03833

Copyright © Denise Lamothe, 2011
All rights reserved

ISBN: 1461111625
ISBN-13: 9781461111627
Library of Congress Control Number: 2011906264

Interior photos by Elizabeth Arnold
Cartoon images by Constance Maines

For Betsy

My partner, who has loved and believed
in me for more years than I can remember

Table of Contents

Table of Contents

GREETINGS!

Allow me to introduce myself…
I am your Appetite.
I may look sinister but I will soon become your best friend.
You'll see!

Preface

This is a book for you and about you. It is about how you have been victimized in today's culture. Perhaps you were urged to mold yourself into a shape that you would never be able to achieve. Maybe you were invalidated and learned that your feelings and thoughts were of no importance. Chances are you were humiliated at times and learned to protect yourself by pushing your emotions deep inside. Instead of being taught how absolutely precious you are, you learned that you were faulty in some way. That is not true. You are perfect just as you are. You will never be able to do everything perfectly at all times—that is not the human way—but you are a perfect being nonetheless.

My position is we have all been damaged in some way during our lifetimes. The beautiful light within each of us has been hidden under a blanket of fear. We grow up thinking that we are not good enough, and we work harder to prove our worth to others to garner their approval. We think if we can get others to admire us, we in some way validate ourselves. We search outside of ourselves for direction and approval instead of looking within and trusting ourselves to know what is best. This tactic will never help us blossom into the energetic, joyful spirits we are deep inside.

Each of the six steps explained in this book has been designed to help you understand why you have been behaving as you have and then help you reconnect with your spirit. You are then free to create the life of your personal dreams—a truly delicious life. The word *delicious*, as defined by *Merriam-Webster*, means "affording great pleasure." And your life should be exactly that—a life of pure pleasure.

I will highlight physical, emotional, social, spiritual, and environmental aspects of self-destructive behavior and offer possible suggestions for change. What you choose to do with this information is unique to you. There is no one answer, no one right way. You are a distinct being—precious and loveable. My hope is you will realize just how magnificent you truly are!

—Dr. Denise Lamothe

Acknowledgments

As with any monumental effort, this work would never have been created without the assistance, love, and support of so many people.

First, I would like to thank Betsy Arnold, my partner, for her patience and help. She selflessly offered her computer assistance skills, her support, and her encouragement. I could not have done this without her!

My deepest appreciation to my wonderful friends, Joan and Digger Day, for letting me hide out at their beautiful, secluded, peaceful camp to write and reflect in the company of many songbirds, hummingbirds, chipmunks, and loons.

Thank you to my precious children and grandchildren, for making me laugh and helping me to remember what is really important in my life, and to my mother, Louise Lamothe, and my sister, Suzanne Nance, for your constant love and support.

Big thank-you hugs to my faithful editors, Mary Lou Fuller and Kay Amsden, who never failed to take what I had written and make it so much more clear, vibrant, and compelling.

My warmest thanks to the many people who spent hours reviewing my work and offering constructive feedback: Elson Haas, Rebecca Rule, Pete Martino, Steve Gamlin, Wayne Cunningham,

Mimi Sorg, Rich DiGirolamo, Sheri Donica, Elaine Schubert, Debby Adair, Maralyn Morrissey, and Adele Robertson.

Much appreciation to Steve and Bill Harrison, Geoffrey Berwin, and all the staff and members of the Quantum Leap Program, for their endless patience, wisdom, and encouragement.

I am also grateful to my Jigsaw Consulting partners, Debby Adair, Steve Gamlin, and Pete Martino, who are always there for me to give me what I need at the time, be it love and support, a pat on the back, or thoughtful suggestions and feedback.

Thanks to Marilee Driscoll for being my friend and spending time brainstorming titles with me. I so much appreciate you for your creativity and quick mind.

Biggest hugs and thank-you pats to my little therapy dog, Sapphi, for taking me on walks, making me play ball, faithfully listening to me, not talking back, and giving me the unconditional love I needed so often throughout this adventure.

Last, but definitely not least, thank you to all of the remarkable clients who have passed through my office doors in the last twenty-plus years. Without your inspiring stories and your willingness to share yourselves with me, this book could not be.

About the Author

Dr. Lamothe, widely known as Dr. Denise, helps people understand emotional aspects of overeating and teaches ways to overcome psychological, emotional, and spiritual roadblocks to permanent weight loss and radiant health. She provides the tools necessary for people to empower themselves and make self-loving choices regarding their lifestyles without judging their behaviors. Let her gently guide you as you chart your own intuitive course to vibrant health.

Dr. Denise served on the team of Ann Louise Gittleman, the "First Lady of Nutrition" and author of over twenty-five best-selling books, including The *Fat Flush* series, and is now a recommended resource for Dr. Gittleman. Dr. Denise also has served as the resident psychologist and professional spokesperson for Bach® Original Flower Remedies.

She is an international professional speaker, author, clinical psychologist, and doctor of holistic health who maintains a thriving practice while speaking and promoting her work. She runs retreats, therapy groups, classes and workshops and treats individual clients in her office or via telephone. In addition, Dr. Denise is an executive and founding member of Jigsaw Consulting, a team of four professional speakers who provide excellent, inspiring seminars, workshops, and writings for organizations, associations, and private groups.

For years, Dr. Denise battled with anorexia, bulimia, binge eating disorder, and finally, extreme obesity before forging her own path to health and balance. She rose above the adversities of being a college dropout, homeless street person, and single mother of three to achieve great success in her field. She is the founder of Emotional Overeating Awareness Month and is the go-to person for people who desire permanent healthy weight loss through the recognition and intuitive understanding of their own unique physical, emotional, and spiritual needs.

Dr. Denise is a member of the American Psychological Association, the National Speakers Association, and the New England Chapter of the National Speakers Association. She currently resides and practices in Exeter, New Hampshire, with her West Highland terrier and therapy dog, Sapphi.

SAPPHI

Foreword

Dr. Denise Lamothe has done it again! Her latest work, *The Appetite Connection*, is a compelling book that finally exposes not only common causes of food obsession, but offers six practical, powerful, and effective steps we can take to permanently stop the self-destructive cycle of overeating. At this critical time when obesity is of pandemic proportions, her work brings hope along with valuable suggestions for real change. Dr. Denise is unique. She addresses the whole picture of self-destructive eating from physical, emotional, social, spiritual, and environmental perspectives. She clarifies many of the reasons for overeating and then delivers a wide range of suggestions to help us understand and reverse this behavior.

From the start of this revolutionary work, Dr. Denise wisely advises us that diets cause weight gain and cautions us never to diet again. Her words of wisdom encourage us to move forward and empower ourselves to live lives of balance, radiant health, and joy—free from food worries. She begins by sharing the compelling stories of eleven former clients who each share a variety of situations they coped with as children and young adults that ultimately led them to eating difficulties later in life. Dr. Denise hits the mark as she addresses these many possible childhood situations—being invalidated, experiencing physical, emotional, or sexual abuse, feeling "not good enough," or being raised in an environment that didn't make sense—that potentially lead to disordered eating.

She summarizes the issues contained in these stories and effectively illuminates many of the reasons we may overeat as adolescents and adults. It is then, armed with this understanding, that we can move forward in our healing process. The understanding gleaned from these powerful stories equips us to shift our attention from our negative past behaviors into a new way of thinking and conquer imbalances in all aspects of our lives, not only eating behaviors.

Dr. Denise discusses the importance of letting go of our impossible desire to be perfect and explains that each of us is already perfect just as we are, but being human means we can never behave perfectly at all times. She also astutely points out that there can be benefits to being overweight. She provides a good example of this and invites us to explore this novel concept in our own life.

Throughout this book, Dr. Denise counsels us to look deep within ourselves for answers. She provides us with tons of suggestions, all the while reminding us to take what fits for us and to discard the rest. She believes that only we know what is in our own best interests and that if we pay attention to the messages our feelings are constantly delivering to us, we can and will make the wisest choices. Dr. Denise names our feelings as our "internal guidance system" and urges us to slow down and pay attention to whatever we are experiencing at the time. She advises us that these feelings are delivering important, empowering messages and that it is our job to listen and heed the inner wisdom our feelings are constantly delivering to us.

Dr. Denise reminds us that there are no mistakes, only lessons, and that we have much to learn from every experience. Her tone is powerful and strong, yet gentle and always nonjudgmental. She is persuasive as she urges us to befriend ourselves, our appetites, and our feelings and informs us that only when we become friendly and gentle with ourselves will we be able to stop the self-harming behavior of overeating once and for all.

At one point, Dr. Denise effectively uses the metaphor of capturing, taming, and then training a wild horse as a way of explaining how to train our appetite, which can feel wild and out of control at times, to work with us instead of against us. As she walks us through the process of taming and then training our horse, she cleverly connects each step to the process of taming and then training our appetite.

She also delves into the importance of communicating clearly and discovering the power deep within each of us. This book is peppered with interesting, colorful personal and professional stories to help us internalize her important messages. Dr. Denise doesn't focus directly on ways to stop unhealthy eating; instead, she guides us there by encouraging us to be courageous and creative. She explains ways to soothe and balance emotions so we may enjoy ourselves instead of living our lives feeling tense and fearful of food.

Scattered throughout *The Appetite Connection* are useful tips to help us cement the many words of wisdom found in each section. This is definitely a hands-on book that you will want to personalize. It is a book to write in, highlight, and keep. It is not a book to skim through and pass on.

Dr. Denise guides us through a step-by-step process of drafting a personal recovery plan that will exactly meet our individual needs. This is a flexible plan we can use every day to transform self-destructive behaviors into powerful, positive life-steps. She concludes her book by urging each of us to make a firm commitment to ourselves, stating that without paying attention to this important step, we are likely to move away from the wisdom we have gained and return to our previous frustrating, self-defeating behaviors.

This book is powerful, entertaining, and enlightening and is finally a book that truly delivers what it promises—*Six Steps to Your Delicious Life and The Body You Long For.*

— Ann Louise Gittleman, PhD, CNS

Introduction

Most of us acknowledge that our bodies and our lives are not as vibrant and energetic as we would like them to be, and millions of us have, in some way, been victimized by the diet industry. In desperation, we have bought and used diet products or weight-loss equipment and helped to create this multi-billion dollar weight loss business. The public, including men, but particularly women, have spent their money freely on diet pills and gimmicks; low-fat, low-calorie, and/or low-carbohydrate diet foods; weight-loss program fees; gym memberships; workout equipment; and personal trainers—all without improving body image, creating a positive relationship with food, or achieving a healthy weight.

Americans have earned the distinction of being the fattest people on earth. As we become more and more aware of this fact, we search desperately for the latest diet. Nearly everyone wants to be thinner, and each new diet offers promise of a slender, strong, and healthy body. Yet, as Americans diet more rigorously, the numbers on their scales continue to rise. Why is this? It is because diets do not work! They actually cause weight gain!

Diets make us fatter in many ways. They DO! They forbid us to eat the healthy fats we require to feel satisfied, they lower our metabolisms, and encourage us to consume diet products that are often full of chemicals and devoid of nutritional value. Diets also foster a lifestyle of deprivation, and if we severely restrict our caloric intake and deny ourselves the pleasure of savoring foods we love, we build resentment. If our friends are enjoying pasta and sauce, while we are unhappily picking at a pathetic bit of broiled chicken and a few leaves of lettuce, we will almost certainly make up for this later by eating to excess—and we won't be choosing more lettuce and chicken.

As each of us searches for the best ways to care for ourselves and our bodies, we can educate ourselves about what foods promote energy and health and choose these most of the time, while allowing ourselves opportunities to indulge now and then. This becomes one of our primary goals as we move toward a delicious life of zest and health.

Seeking instant gratification leads to overeating, followed by punishing periods of deprivation. We starve ourselves and then stuff our bodies until we fall upon our beds at night like beached whales. It is definitely time for a change. It's time to take charge of our bodies and ourselves because our old patterns have not gotten us very far, have they?

I strongly suggest you stop supporting the "diet gimmick" industry right this minute. I will share many secrets of success, and you will be empowered to forge your own path to a positive self-image, high level of self-respect, and well-being. If you read carefully and implement some of the suggestions in this book, you will feel happy, healthy, and whole. That is my absolute promise to you!

The Appetite Connection educates and entertains you, while gently, but firmly, assisting you to take charge of your situation and make necessary physical, emotional, social, environmental, attitudinal, and spiritual adjustments to live more joyfully and productively— no longer restricted by ill-health, failures, guilt, sadness, and fear.

Changing your diet mindset, releasing your need to be perfect, nurturing your spirit, and learning how to communicate with your Appetite and training it to work *with* you instead of *against* you are the final steps you need to take to put this issue of weight control behind you once and for all. You deserve this. You have struggled long enough!

Introduction

At times, I will refer to your "Chew," which I wrote about in my first book, *The Taming of the Chew*. The following is a brief explanation of the Chew for those of you who may not be familiar with this term, followed by an overview of what *The Appetite Connection* will provide for you. Reading this prepares you to embark on your exciting healing journey.

Our Chew, which I shall also refer to as our Appetite, is our saboteur and is always ready to sabotage our most sincere and ambitious attempts to stop eating compulsively. The Chew is not a stranger to the millions of us who have struggled with food-control issues for a lifetime.

Please approach this experience one day at a time and with an open mind. Suspend any expectations you now hold about your eating behavior. It has taken you years to become a compulsive eater. Your Appetite has been in charge for a long while, and it will take time to reverse old, self-destructive behaviors. Be patient and gentle with yourself as you discover the power of your Appetite Connection.

As you become more familiar with yourself and learn to use your internal guidance system, you will be able to heed the messages of your Appetite before you reach for the cookies. You can then maintain control over yourself, your eating behavior, and your life. You *can* live free from insistent urges to binge. Wait and see!

I will show you how by explaining and simplifying the six necessary steps and by providing you with guidance along the way that enables you to incorporate what you have read into your life to finally free yourself of worries about food control and your body.

Permanent weight loss is one benefit of reading this book and following the suggestions that appeal to you. But you discover other important benefits as well. You empower yourself to create radiant health and well-being. You begin to identify and express your feelings to adjust your attitude, build greater self-confidence, eliminate negative self talk and create success. You learn step-by-step ways to craft a personal self-care plan to meet your own individual needs, and you naturally find yourself rekindling your spirit of creativity and fun. You begin to experience a vibrant, delicious life of balance and joy!

As clients in my practice have, you will recognize your own struggles in the case studies presented and be gently encouraged to make modifications that enable you to improve your life. You learn ways to identify and communicate your feelings because it has, in part, been the lack of honest expression of these feelings that has enticed you into the overeating trap in the past. Finally you are urged to honor yourself and make a serious commitment to your self-care.

You DO NOT need another diet book. After reading this book and implementing some of the suggestions, you will have the understanding and skills necessary to put this issue to rest. You must understand what you are doing and believe that you are not crazy or a failure; you have been doing your best with the confusing messages you have been receiving about how to lose weight, maintain weight loss, and be proud of yourself. This book validates your experience. The goal throughout is to help you feel good about yourself as you learn to use your internal, intuitive guidance system to choose your own standards for your health and well-being and set the stage for health living.

My wish for you is that you discover that your Appetite, which in the past has represented a frustrating, hurtful part of yourself, can now become helpful. Although in the past it has worked against your own best interests, it can now actually help you move away from your years of pain and frustration to arrive at a place of confidence, pride, and wellness.

I became a victim of the dangerous diet industry at age ten. I was anorexic for several years, bulimic for seven more, then ate compulsively and became extremely obese for many years after that. Binge eating was my lifestyle. I am only one of millions of casualties spread around our globe, and the business of enticing us to lose weight has grown by leaps and bounds. I have watched as others have cried in frustration and have listened to their painful stories. They have shared not only their experiences, but those of their children and grandchildren as well. What has been going on in our country for generations now is heartbreaking and dangerous.

The Appetite Connection will encourage and empower you if you too are one of the millions of us who have battled with losing and maintaining our ideal healthy weight. It teaches you to distinguish emotional from physical eating and guides you through a step-by-step process of letting go of traditional diet restriction techniques. You learn to train your Appetite to work with you in your best interests by focusing within yourself and using your intuition to outline specific, effective ways to achieve the physical and emotional balance necessary for living a joyful life.

You are about to transform your approach to all aspects of your life. As you read each page, your focus expands so that instead of merely considering food control and weight loss or maintenance, you think of yourself in the total context of your life. Then you are able to craft the life you desire, not simply in areas of eating and body size, but in its entirety.

You are already aware that diets eventually result in weight gain, but you have had no knowledge of how to manage your weight without restrictive dieting. You have been seeking a better, healthier way to manage your eating behavior and find peace and balance in your life, but perhaps you have lacked the skills necessary to be successful. You have had the right idea, but no solution. This has not been your fault.

As an emotional overeating expert and weight-loss strategist who has spent over twenty-five years counseling individuals with food-control problems through therapy sessions, writings, public talks, and workshops, I have found that most people, mainly women, are confused and hold fast to the perfectionistic self-expectations that have led them to fail. I will discuss this in detail to help you stop positioning yourself to fail by setting unattainable goals. This is critically important, because if you continually feel like a failure, you will assuredly choose sugar, simple carbohydrates, fat and salt to soothe yourself. This type of emotional overeating, as you know so well, leads to weight gain, followed by more guilt, more eating, and more weight gain, followed by more guilt, more eating, and so on—a cycle so many of us have repeated again and again. (This was my lifestyle for many, many years!)

If you have been searching for answers, I've got some. This issue is complex, and there is much to understand. It may seem overwhelming now, but I break the issue of overeating down into small, easy-to-understand segments (bite-sized pieces) for you and address each aspect separately.

One of the reasons so many of us struggle with these issues is that we are people who want magic answers and instant gratification. We want what we want right now! You will need to bypass your urges to tear through this book. Please slow down. This is not easy for many of us, but I promise you going slowly, being thoughtful, and taking one step at a time will definitely pay off.

You will never be told what to do. You will never be judged. Instead, you will be repeatedly encouraged to look within yourself for your own answers and you will be taught step by step exactly how to do so. All I ask is that you read and consider the information I provide. Adopt what is useful to you. Take what fits and discard the rest.

Far too many well-meaning people put forth theories and suggest actions in general ways, as if one size fits all or one suggestion is the right one for everyone. Well, one size definitely does not fit all. One method of self-care may work beautifully for your friend, but may not be helpful for you. You will require a unique plan because you are an individual and your needs do not exactly match those of anyone else.

Your Appetite may appear to be an insatiable adversary that pushes you towards the desert table and urges you to eat with wild abandon but you and your Appetite can connect and become a team of two working together to combat overeating urges. You will be super heros battling the urges together that have so often caused you pain and suffering in the past. Hard to imagine? Read on!

For the Male Reader

This book is written for you as well as for the thousands of women with whom I have worked. Many of you have come through my office door voicing the same concerns as my female clients. We are different genders, but we all share similar frustrations and common concerns. We have all been victimized by the food and diet industries. I write this book using female pronouns almost exclusively simply because it makes the writing easier. If I had to use he/she and him/her as I wrote, it would have been impossibly tedious and made the book difficult to write and read.

Therefore, I ask that you overlook the pronouns and take what fits for you from the contents. If you are struggling with issues about your body image and your weight, this book is as much for you as it is for any woman. Most of the content is not gender-specific. Some parts do directly address women, as we are socialized differently from you.

As I always stress to my readers, please take from this work what fits and discard the rest. My wish is that this book helps you to forge your own unique path to happiness, radiant health, and balance.

THE SIX STEPS

STEP I – Understand Why You Overeat

What was it that led you down the self-destructive path of eating problems? Are you the only one on this planet who struggles in this way, or do others share your pain? Do you realize how your early development set the stage for your behavior today? Do you recognize the links between your early experiences and the ways in which you are impacted today by what occurred in your formative years? Do you wonder about the psychology behind your actions today? Most women have little to no knowledge of how they initially got involved with food-control issues. Do you?

In this chapter we consider these questions to help you understand how you have arrived at this time in your life with food problems still so difficult or seemingly impossible. We look to the past in order to move ahead into a healthy future unencumbered by these questions and those old, guilty, frustrated feelings.

In order to truly heal from food-control problems, it is necessary for you to have a basic appreciation of how you got to where you are. Once you achieve a general understanding of your past, you can transform your unhealthy behaviors into ones that are life affirming, productive, and healthy. It is confusing to attempt changes without knowing how your behaviors began. Demystifying the impact your past has had, and continues to have, will enable you to let the past go and move forward. We all have emotional issues that stem from experiences during our early years. We cannot erase them, but we can understand, forgive where necessary, and move on to create the life we desire and deserve.

In my experience, most women are quick to cast blame on themselves for their failure to manage their eating by saying they have no willpower or are "bad" for not controlling themselves. As you will see, this is faulty thinking. Within the stories I present to you in Step I, you will discover possible reasons for your food-control problems, and then in the following steps, you will be given many workable solutions. As you continue, you will change on many levels—cognitively, emotionally, physically, and spiritually. I urge you to move slowly through each chapter and think carefully about what you are reading.

Later, you are guided and encouraged to make your own flexible plan. You design this plan for your personal use. It will be tailored to meet your individual needs as they change over time and serves as a map to guide you along your personal path to happiness, health, and balance. You will be able to consult your plan as often as you like—daily or even more often than that—as you make decisions about your lifestyle and eating behavior. It serves as your anchor as you negotiate the challenges of each day.

You finally conquer emotional overeating. Yo-yo numbers reflected on the scale stabilize. You feel confident, and in control of all aspects of your health and well-being. You create the delicious life of balance and joy you desire and deserve.

To accomplish this, it helps to glance back into your past to get a general idea of how your food problems began. I am not suggesting we spend a great deal of time considering or discussing childhood experiences, as it is not productive to keep the focus of your attention on the past. It is only useful to gain a general understanding and then use your new awareness to enhance your life in the present. This helps you move forward smoothly, with greater confidence and power. Ignorance breeds confusion, and in order to make the constructive changes you want, you need to be fully aware.

It is important, however, to seek the services of a counseling professional if you have past experiences and feelings that are interfering with your life activities. For example, if you were abused as a child, you may need to talk about it or even confront your abuser. This may be therapeutic. Or if you have suffered great loss and are feeling mired in sadness and grief, you may want to talk with a caring, trained professional to resolve these feelings and thereby free yourself to move on. It is imperative that you do not remain stuck in the past. Obtain the guidance you need to release the past and make yourself and your present life number one on your priority list.

It is critical that you have a plan in place. If you are in Florida and want to drive to Maine, you might never make it without a map and plan of action. You would head in an unknown direction looking for a sign that you were getting closer to Maine. You could end up in California or North Dakota that way. To achieve your goal of proceeding directly to Maine, you need to have a plan. With a clear set of directions in hand, the route is easy. It will take a while, but since you are prepared for the distance, you will progress patiently along your route knowing that you will eventually arrive at your desired destination.

This initial section gives you the understanding you need to begin. Then the book gives you information you need to draw the best map for yourself. Finally, as you make your personal plan (or map), you will be off on your trip to vibrant health, joy, radiance, and your delicious life!

Let me explain how this initial chapter can help you. You could read every psychology book ever written that addresses eating problems, traditionally called eating disorders. There are hundreds, but why would you want to spend precious hours doing so? Most likely, you don't have the extra time this effort would require, and you would read theories that often contradict each other, digging up a great deal of confusing, erroneous information. You could end up more perplexed than you were in the first place. You would most likely be even more frustrated and discouraged than when you began your quest for radiant health. Without clear directions, finding solutions is impossible. You could remain mired in confusion for the rest of your life.

In "Understand Why You Overeat," I tell you some typical stories designed to help you learn the basics of some of the psychology behind eating problems in an interesting and informative way. I share the composite experiences of eleven men and women with whom I have worked during the past twenty-five years. The names are changed and their identities carefully guarded. Any resemblance to anyone you know is clearly coincidental, as the details of each person's situation have been substantially altered.

I have noticed in my practice that there are certain common factors in the backgrounds of most of the people who seek my services. As you read these stories, you are likely to recognize aspects of your own life in one or more of the case studies. Perhaps you will see yourself in a number of them. It is OK if you do not identify with any. We are all different, and there are no situations that apply to everyone. We all do what we do because of factors too numerous to identify. What is essential is your willingness to look within yourself as you move forward. On this journey, you will increase self-awareness and view yourself and your behavior differently. Then you will be empowered to give up some of the damaging aspects of your past to create the life you want.

Some of the common factors we will consider include women and men who:

- have been victims of physical, emotional, and/or sexual abuse. (Erin)

- set perfection as their goal. (Michelle)

- were raised in a disconnected, chaotic family. (Zoe)

- were the black sheep in their family. (Martin)

- grew up with mothers who had food-control problems. (Jane)

- were caretakers of siblings, parents, and others. (Susie)

- learned that focusing on approval reduces stress and gets attention. (Paula)

- were overachievers. (Mike)

- had a low level of self-esteem and saw themselves as powerless. (Jill)

- learned that extra weight could give them an advantage. (Mia)

- were overprotected by their caregivers. (Sally)

Note: You may be tempted to skip over this section on how your eating issues began. I strongly suggest you resist that urge. The following case studies help you identify possible ways you were set up for eating problems as a child. Arming yourself with this valuable information helps you move rapidly along your path to a peaceful mind and a vibrant, healthy, glowing body. It is up to you. If you are not interested in reading these stories before you begin, please read the summary that follows the stories, skip to Step II, and return to this section later. <u>Please don't forget to return, however, because your history will continue to influence you and how you care for yourself until you can understand it and let go.</u>

...and now, The Stories

Erin — who suffered physical, emotional and sexual abuse

Erin grew up in a large family. She had three older brothers and one little sister, and she loved her siblings very much. The family lived on a large farm, and she recalled her love for the land and the many animals in residence on their property. She delighted in watching sunrises and feeding the little chickens as they pecked around the barnyard. She recalled one very special pet—a little, brown, scruffy dog named Casey, whom she remembered cuddling and talking to when things were difficult. She credited Casey's devotion for her ability to survive repeated, brutal abuse throughout her childhood years.

The trouble started when Erin was about seven years old. Prior to that time, she remembered being quite close to her father, helping him with farm chores, gathering eggs, and riding behind him on his John Deere tractor. She was not sure what caused the change, but after the summer of her seventh year, things were never the same.

Erin's father began drinking, and she described their relationship as becoming distant. This confused her because she craved the attention and approval he had given her in the past. Unfortunately, her father was unable to manage the many stressors of farm life without his nightly drinks, and his personality soon changed. The once loving father she adored became a man she did not know. He was cruel to her, her mother, and her siblings. She didn't understand why this change had taken place. Erin secretly wondered if she had somehow caused the dramatic change in her father's behavior and remembered him drinking every night and having frequent, violent fights with her mother and her older brothers.

One memory Erin shared was of her father shouting at her mother, hitting her, and shoving her across the living room. One of her older brothers tried to intervene to protect their mother, but her father was bigger and stronger and punched her brother, who fell sobbing to the floor, covering his head to protect himself from further damaging blows. She recalled hiding upstairs, holding her little sister in her arms. She covered the baby's ears in an attempt to block out her father's shouting and her mother's screams. After that night, her brothers would disappear whenever the fights started, and she had no idea where they went. She was left alone with her little sister, and she had to protect herself and the baby. She had no memory of anyone ever helping her, standing up for her, or protecting her.

After these horrible, explosive episodes subsided, the house would usually be quiet for a week or so, and Erin would stow a little dog cookie or two in her pocket, take Casey, and head out through the lush fields and woods. She would give Casey a treat and lie in the grass with him snuggled next to her and watch as the clouds floated by. This little corner of the field became an oasis for her. During these peaceful times, she would dream and imagine a better life and a happier family, with a loving, patient, and concerned father—the father she remembered from her earliest years. She couldn't understand why her father had become so mean or why her mother would put up with his abusive behavior. She tried not to think about it. Life was confusing enough! Instead, she focused her attention on Casey's warm, soft fur and daydreamed her way back to a peaceful mood.

Time passed and Erin's situation grew dramatically worse. Her mother, who had seemed sad and apathetic ever since Erin could remember, became severely depressed and was hospitalized for a time. She couldn't recall how long her mother was gone from home, but because she was the oldest daughter, many of her mother's duties were delegated to her. So, as a young girl, she assumed responsibility for the care and feeding of her father, her brothers, and her little sister.

Although this was an inappropriate role for an eight-year-old, especially in addition to Erin's academic responsibilities, she didn't mind the added burdens placed on her—at least not at first. There were no more frightening, nighttime battles between her father and mother. Her father continued his nightly drinking ritual, however, and soon started arguing with her brothers. These arguments most often ended violently, with her father beating her brothers (when he could catch them). It seemed to Erin that her father would criticize her brothers unnecessarily and create reasons to punish them. Once Erin tried to intervene on her brothers' behalf, and her dad slapped her because she dared to speak up. She became even more confused and upset. She felt worried about her mother and powerless to manage the conflict in her home. The abuse continued to escalate, and there was no one around to help her or her siblings. She never felt safe, and she began to worry all the time. Even time spent with Casey didn't console her as it once had.

Late one night, her father came quietly into the bedroom, and Erin, although half asleep, was aware that he was standing over her bed watching her. In some way, she sensed this was a dangerous situation. She kept her eyes shut and pretended to be asleep. Her heart was racing, her stomach was upset, and she didn't even know what she was afraid of. It wasn't long before she found out.

Eventually, Erin's father came to her room nightly. At first, he would sit on the edge of the bed and stroke her back and shoulders. She remembers feeling too scared to speak. She would lie perfectly still and continue to pretend she was asleep, praying that each time would be the last time. For many years, he came to her bed with his sour, alcoholic breath and his rough farm hands. He touched her and kissed her. She would lie still and stare at the flowers on her wallpaper, praying her father would soon finish what he was doing and leave the room. Each time he told her she was special and that his nightly visits were their little secret. He threatened to hurt her precious Casey and abuse her little sister instead of her if she ever told anyone about their "special" relationship. Erin was helpless and terrified. Her grades dropped, and she stopped enjoying the activities she once loved.

When her mother returned home, Erin prayed the abuse would stop. She felt dirty and helpless and just wanted her mother to come to her rescue, but she couldn't bring herself to tell her mother what was going on. Erin was afraid her mother wouldn't believe her and wondered if the abuse was somehow her fault. She also feared that her father would shoot Casey or abuse her little sister, whom she felt responsible for and was very protective of.

It made no positive difference when Erin's mother returned from the hospital. Things got worse instead of better. Her father not only continued his nightly visits, but also began seeking out Erin during the day. He would order her to go to the barn, where he would kiss and touch her. Erin became more and more withdrawn. She bit her fingernails until they bled. She sneaked food from the pantry. The cookies and pastries she stole and ate in secret soothed her for a while, but when the sugar rush wore off, she would hunt for more—pasta, Jell-O powder, ice cream, anything she could find in an attempt to anesthetize herself from the feelings of misery and despair.

Erin gained weight rapidly. She waited impatiently for the day she could move out and be on her own. She imagined that once she was away and free, she would find the happiness she craved. At age eighteen, she began dating Al. They talked about marriage, and she soon ran away with her husband-to-be. They settled into a small apartment near his family, and Erin thought she could put the past behind her. As the years passed, however, Erin continued her out-of-control eating. The harder she tried to lose weight, the more weight she gained. By the time she came into my office, Erin was dangerously overweight, extremely depressed, anxious, and frustrated. She feared that she would never be able to reverse her self-destructive behavior and come to peaceful terms with her body. Erin shared her painful history with me. As she talked, she began to realize that what had happened in her family was in no way her fault and that she had behaved in the only way she could in order to survive. She was able to view herself not only as a victim of circumstance, but as a strong, vibrant woman who had survived a dreadful time in her life. It is not, and never will be, acceptable that Erin was treated in this way, but she was able to realize that dwelling on the past would prevent her from moving forward. Coming to terms with her past was the only way to change old, negative patterns into productive, healthy ones. We spent months sorting out her thoughts and feelings about her early years until she was able to take giant steps toward creating a healthy mind and body.

Many women who come to see me talk of substance abuse in their families and various ways in which they were abused—physically, emotionally, and/or sexually. I find that most, as with Erin, have been abused in all three ways. Acknowledging this and moving forward is empowering; staying stuck in the past is not. It can be helpful to seek counseling with a professional, but it is equally important to move on and create a healthier life as soon as you can.

Michelle – who thought she had to be perfect

Michelle was an attractive, intelligent businesswoman. She was head of human resources for a large company, exceptionally good at her job, and always striving to improve her performance and her appearance. She described herself as an overachiever and said she had been this way as long as she could remember. Michelle grew up in a small family. Her mother and father were both involved in prestigious careers. Michelle's father was a noted physician in their community, and her mother was a real estate agent who worked long hours and had built a very successful and profitable business.

She had an older brother named Bruce, whom she adored. When she was in grammar school, he would take her with him and his friends to attend a movie after school or go out for french fries and milk shakes at the corner snack shop. Michelle recalled these outings as the very best times of her childhood.

When she entered high school, her brother went away to college. She missed him totally. Although they talked weekly by phone, she was sad and lonely and was left to fend for herself after school. She soon learned that the busier she became, the less she missed Bruce.

Michelle launched herself into high school full force. She was a straight-A student and got involved in many school activities. She was in the drama club and was usually assigned the lead in school productions. Michelle was a star. Everyone said so. She dressed in the latest fashions and was praised for her achievements. The more she did, the more she was praised; therefore, she continued to do more and more until her life began spiraling out of control and she was unable to relax.

Michelle found herself eating to soothe her anxiety. She was fearful she would let her parents and her brother down if she was less than perfect. If you set perfection as your goal, you are guaranteed to fail. Michelle knows that now, but she didn't then. She continued to soothe her anxiety with food and, consequently, began to gain weight. She became more and more upset as the numbers on the scale rose, but she felt powerless to stop. The more weight she gained, the more anxious she felt and the more she ate. To keep the numbers on the scale from rising too fast, she would alternate between overeating and starving herself. She was trapped in this self-defeating cycle for years, hiding her pain from everyone around her.

Michelle kept a big smile on her face, continued to dress fashionably, and earned an A+ in each class at school. She appeared to be perfect on the outside. She was of average weight (although she viewed herself as fat), active, and involved in numerous activities. She appeared calm and in control on the outside, but inside, Michelle was suffering. She had everyone fooled, but the stress was taking a toll.

When she was fifteen years old, Michelle went on her first diet. As she matured, bulges appeared here and there. The image of her body in the mirror was distorted as she saw her overweight reflection. She was terrified and feared she would get larger and larger. Being overweight did not fit with her image of perfection, and she felt out of control. She became more and more desperate and frantically continued her efforts to lose weight.

Michelle starved herself, took diet pills, and ate cabbage soup and grapefruit sections. She explored various associations that promised help with weight loss, guidance, and support. She tried programs that sold her special meals and other programs where she was weighed each week. The harder she tried to lose weight, the more she gained, and the further she got from her image of perfection. She exercised feverishly and increased her extracurricular activities. Her focus became her body. The harder she worked to correct her weight, the more she gained. It was a vicious cycle—one that millions of people are caught up in every day.

Instead of having fun and enjoying her life, Michelle's mood darkened, and she began to isolate herself. She imagined herself as fat and as a failure, and she became paranoid, imagining that others were negatively judging her appearance. It was increasingly difficult for Michelle to maintain her image of perfection. Her parents and friends noticed her change in behavior and worried as her moods became more erratic. She was scared and ashamed. She didn't understand what was going on, and she refused to communicate with anyone. Her brother tried to talk with her about her condition, but she even refused to talk with him.

She denied that her drive for perfection was the leading cause behind her distress. She didn't understand the connection between her need to be perfect and her deteriorating condition. Michelle admitted she would never have expected of anyone else what she expected of herself. Her goals were unattainable, and her constant search for perfection doomed her to fail.

Michelle's fears of failure stemmed from her sadness at the loss of her brother and her desire to please her parents and show them she was the perfect daughter. She craved their approval and attention. Because they both worked long hours and had much of their energy invested in their own careers, they had never been accessible to Michelle.

There is no way to know if Michelle's issues would have developed had her brother not left for college or if her environment had been different. Her parents did love her, and they demonstrated this in many ways. They provided a beautiful home and all possible material goods, and they paid attention to her whenever they could. They loved her deeply, but because she appeared to be doing so well, they weren't really concerned. They had no reason to be.

Michelle, however, craved approval. She imagined that if she were perfect, she would garner more attention and would know she was lovable. It was impossible for her to imagine that she was already perfect and lovable. I see this often. Women fear that something is wrong with them, and they expect to behave perfectly in every situation. They strive to look beautiful at all times, with not a hair out of place. They appear to be communicating openly with their friends and family, when, in actuality, they paste smiles on their faces, while inside they are crying and feeling deep sadness.

Food serves as a buffer from the stress people feel. The battle between needing to be perfect and needing to be human is pulling them apart. Generally, they both blame themselves and beat themselves up when they eat something that they view as "bad" food. They report feeling out of control and say things such as, "I have my whole life in order, but I can't seem to get a grip on this eating issue. If I could just get this one thing under control, my life would be perfect." As they come to realize the futility of seeking perfection and discover they are perfect and lovable as they are, they begin to relax, their food issues recede, and they are able to move in a healthier direction.

Michelle spent months working to stop her unrealistic, perfectionistic demands. It wasn't until she really understood the link between her self-imposed mandate to be perfect and her emotional eating behavior that she was able to relax and allow herself to have fun. She began striving for balance and health instead of being focused on having the perfect body, the perfect weight, and the perfect life.

Zoe – who grew up in a crazy, chaotic environment

A t our initial meeting, Zoe happily announced that her family was perfect and that she had had a perfect childhood. At least she thought this was true. She said her father and mother appeared to adore each other, their marriage seemed stable, and the family had lots of friends who came by for parties and visits. Her father worked long hours as a dedicated engineer in a large company. Her mother was a stay-at-home mom devoted to her family. Zoe was painting a picture of the ideal family.

Her mother loved to entertain, and Zoe was frequently asked to help with planning, decorating, serving the meal, and cleaning up after the guests had departed. These occasions were festive, and everyone seemed to have a good time. Zoe didn't feel as happy as everyone else seemed to be, and she thought something was wrong with her for being less than enthusiastic about these events. She remembered the countless evenings of entertaining that her mother orchestrated and the endless stream of guests in and out of her home.

The family lived in a lovely sprawling ranch house in an elite suburb of an affluent community. The relationships that Zoe observed appeared to be perfect—that is, everyone seemed to be happy and content. She secretly thought they were not quite so happy inside, but she really didn't know. All she knew was that *she* wasn't as happy as everyone else seemed to be. She was convinced she must be flawed in some important way to be so moody and discontent.

Zoe and her sister and brother went to the best school in the area. It was a private, exclusive school, and Zoe recalled feeling challenged by the academic expectations that all of the students experienced. She tried hard to excel and did do well, earning very high grades in all of her classes. She was a member of the debate club and the drama club as well as the captain of the cheerleading squad throughout high school. She admitted that she was an overachiever and didn't mind the constant pressure of her courses and many extracurricular activities. She received much praise and attention at home for her superior academic and athletic efforts.

School was not much fun for Zoe, although she acted as if it were. She had many acquaintances and was popular, but she had few close friends. In certain ways, she did enjoy herself. She loved to dance and dated a young man named Alex for three of her high school years. She and Alex made the picture-perfect couple—each was attractive, smart, and energetic. Their relationship showed promise for the future, and everyone assumed they would marry someday. When Alex decided in the middle of Zoe's senior year to date other girls, she was devastated and recalled that as a particularly painful and sad time.

Zoe remembered family vacations and trips into the city to attend plays and enjoy concerts, dinners in fine restaurants, and memberships at the tennis and golf clubs. Other than suffering through the break-up with Alan, Zoe had what many would refer to as a charmed life—a perfect upbringing in every way. Why then would this young woman who was so loved and ostensibly so well cared for become immersed in eating problems at a young age? Apparently, this was not really such a perfect picture.

The key to this mystery is the word *apparently*. Although all of Zoe's family members played their respective roles beautifully, the reality was they were not authentic and were not connected to one another. Let me explain.

It is vital for each of us to be emotionally connected to those around us. Through the development of Self-in-Relation Theory at the Stone Center, Wellesley College, Wellesley, Massachusetts, we have learned that our self-esteem depends upon our ability to make and maintain growth-promoting, reciprocal connections with others in our lives. In order for us to feel well—to be happy, relaxed, peaceful, and balanced—we need to relate to the people in our families and environments in a way that makes sense to us. We know instinctively if people are not being genuine, if their words and actions do not match their feelings, and when we are aware of this, we often make sense of it by deciding that our perceptions are wrong.

Although we may not have realized it, many of us experienced a disconnection at home as children and were deeply affected by it. This was the case with Zoe. She was taught to smile, to be proper, and to act the part of the perfect daughter while she witnessed those around her playing their own parts in her life drama. For example, feelings of sadness, frustration, or anger were not welcomed in her home. She could only say and express what she imagined she should to fit into a family scene that didn't make sense to her. She thought she was the only one with negative feelings, so she deduced at a young age that something was wrong deep inside of her.

As we talked in her therapy sessions, Zoe began to realize that she was not crazy and that she had been constantly receiving mixed messages throughout her childhood. It became clear to her that she had had no way to make sense of the world around her—the world that appeared to be so perfect. If she was hurt, she turned off her tears, knowing in advance that they would not be tolerated.

If she attempted to talk with her mother about feeling bad in some way, she was told not to feel that way. Instead, she was told to cheer up, smile, and move on. She learned to disregard her true feelings and to instead put an acceptable expression on her face and say only the approved words. Her life, which appeared very good, was indeed very bad.

Zoe learned as a toddler that sugar would calm her nerves and help her feel better. She began stealing food on many occasions. At an early age, she recalled pushing a chair over to the counter, climbing up, and searching in the cupboards for sugar. One day, when she was about five years old, she climbed up on the dining room hutch. Zoe knew that her mother was having dinner guests that evening, and she had seen her put a fancy candy dish, filled with peppermint patties, on a high shelf, intending to put them on the table at the end of the meal. (The details of this experience were as clear to her as if it had just happened. That is an indication of how upsetting it was.)

Because sugar, simple carbohydrates, salt and fat are so addictive and because Zoe felt such a strong need to have some, she snuck into the dining room several times during that day to climb up on the hutch and grab one or two more of the delicious patties. Sometime late in the afternoon, she recalled reaching her tiny hand into the dish and discovering that only two patties remained. She was alarmed but took one more anyway and left the last one in the dish, rationalizing that at least there would be something there when her mother reached for the dish at the end of the meal.

Zoe remembered lying in her bed listening as the dinner guests laughed and enjoyed themselves. She waited with dread for the meal to end and for her mother to reach for the peppermint patties. She prayed that somehow she wouldn't be discovered, but she knew she would be considered the most likely suspect, as she had been caught stealing candy before. Sure enough, the moment she had been anticipating with terror arrived, and she could hear her mother clearing away the dinner dishes. When her mother returned to the dining room she reached for the after-dinner mints. Zoe held her breath and shook with fear under her covers. Then she heard her mother laugh loudly and nervously exclaim, "Well, look at this! Zoe was at it again!"

Zoe did not remember what happened after that. She only remembers being flooded with guilt and shame. At only five years old, she knew something was terribly wrong with her. She had suspected it, but after that night, she knew it was true. She started then on a self-destructive course. She kept trying to make sense of things in a crazy-making home where people were superficial and disconnected. She was sensitive and yearned for connection, but she was unable to find it in her family.

What made this so hard was that everyone else appeared to be happy and she had to internalize all of her true feelings to fit in. Zoe continued to suppress her emotions with sugar, simple carbohydrates, salt and fat and became severely addicted to these substances. This frightened her. She was determined not to gain weight and became filled with conflict about what to eat, how much, and how often. For several years, Zoe was bulimic. She would eat and then vomit and exercise excessively attempting to stay thin and socially acceptable. She admitted to me that she had never been able to relax and enjoy her food.

Throughout her life, Zoe continued her attempts to make sense of her life. She read many self-help books, sought the services of therapists, prayed, and joined a number of support groups. She continued her quest for perfection. She reported that she had difficulties with intimacy later in life, and she and her husband had been attempting to improve their relationship. They had begun seeing a therapist, and Zoe was optimistic that she and her husband would be able to work things out between them.

As long as Zoe remained convinced that something was wrong with her, however, her efforts to find peace, balance, and happiness were futile. It wasn't until she came to understand how she had been affected by the dynamics in her family that she could even consider the possibility that she was, in fact, OK. She recognized that she was the product of a chaotic and confusing family—one that appeared

perfect on the surface but, in reality, was inauthentic and disconnected. She knew this as a child but had no way to make sense of it.

Once she understood, she set out on a new journey—one with
good, honest, and open communication and one with clear boundaries. As she started to make the adjustments necessary to express
her feelings and behave authentically, she began moving toward a
life of balance, health, and joy. She started to feel connected and
secure. Her relationships improved, and her weight stabilized. Her
self-esteem and body image quickly improved, and she was well on
her way to achieving the delicious life she desired.

Martin – who was the black sheep of the family

M artin sounded nervous when he called requesting an appointment. His voice shook, and he stumbled over his words. He couldn't tell me anything that was going on or why he wanted to come in. Clearly, he was reaching out for help. All he could say was he wanted to talk. I scheduled a time for him to come in the following day. He thanked me and hung up, and I was left wondering whether he would actually keep his appointment or if he would back out of this opportunity for therapy.

To my delight and surprise, Martin arrived at my office exactly at the appointed time. He was clean-shaven, well dressed, and offered a firm handshake. This was not what I expected. The shy, nervous voice on the phone the day before did not prepare me for this well-put-together young man. Although Martin was extremely obese, he was a handsome twenty-eight-year-old who seemed comfortable with his size. He appeared confident, and I thought he was either not the same person who had phoned the day before or was putting on a very convincing act. The latter proved to be true.

Martin came into the room and settled into one of the comfortable chairs. My little therapy dog, Sapphi, was in the room and started doing what she does—wildly wagging her tail and doing her best to be cute and welcoming. It worked. Martin was happy and excited to play with her. Sapphi enjoyed it, too, and I could see Martin was having fun. I let the two of them interact for a few minutes, and then I asked Martin if he was ready to talk.

Switching his attention to me, he at first just wanted to talk about my dog. He asked lots of questions about her and her training and recalled that he'd had a little dog similar to Sapphi when he was a boy. Eventually, though, Martin began to talk about himself. He told me he had grown up in a large Irish Catholic family. He had two older sisters and three brothers. Although he felt pretty sure they all cared about each other, he said no one ever shared their feelings, and he didn't feel he could confide in any of them.

His father was a large, burly man who Martin described as "loud, often drunk, and distant." Martin remembered him as someone who usually came home hours after dinnertime smelling of alcohol. His mother, who worked in a local garment factory, was quiet and passive and was the sole caretaker of the children. "Mother always seemed tired," Martin said. He never felt comfortable talking to her; she seemed too sad and lonely herself. When Martin's father arrived home each night, he and Martin's mother barely spoke. If they did, it was often in anger, and Martin's father became loud and belligerent. He yelled at Martin's mother and all the kids, but Martin had no recollection of physical violence.

Martin's father and his brothers were avid fans of the Boston Patriots, the Bruins, and the Red Sox, as were all of their neighbors and most of Martin's relatives. Sports teams and scores were the only topics he recalled being discussed in his home. Not only did everyone profess their love for the Boston sports teams, but they also played these same sports after school and every weekend. His father and brothers were excellent sportsmen. If they weren't at a home game, they were following sports on television. It was expected that all males in the area would flock to the neighborhood bar to cheer on their teams. Martin admitted he was never interested in sports and did not enjoy physical activity, so he hid when they got ready to go to the bar or play outside. He usually fabricated a reason not to join them and busied himself with another chore. Sometimes he stole whatever he could from the kitchen cupboards and retreated to his room to eat.

Martin excelled academically, earning straight A's through grammar school. He told me his grades dropped off in high school and that he always dreaded Thursdays because that was gym-class day. He claimed he hated going into the boys' locker room and putting on his gym shorts, which were too tight. He was not athletic, and he couldn't throw or catch like the others. Martin ran slowly, tripped often, and soon became the brunt of many jokes whenever his classmates were out of earshot of the coach.

Sometimes the other boys would push or shove him or make jokes about his protruding belly and puffy chest. He was called names like "sissy," "mama's boy," or "tank." He told me that he wanted to crawl away and hide and had occasionally wished he were dead. He never concocted a suicide plan and never attempted to hurt himself, but the urges were there nonetheless.

Although Martin had always been slightly "chubby" like everyone else in his family, he found himself gaining more weight as he moved through high school, while his siblings and most of his classmates grew taller and slimmer in their teens. Martin never dated and had few friends. Only one boy, Ted, was really a friend, and they would occasionally go to the movies or the local pizza joint. Martin said he always had enjoyed sweets, but as a teenage boy, his eating became out of control, and he could never get enough of them.

Martin had learned to bury his feelings of inadequacy and shame under mountains of sugary, salty, fatty foods. He worked part time stocking shelves in the neighborhood corner store and used most of his earnings to buy bags of candy and cookies. He hid them and consumed them whenever no one else was around to witness his binges. He even recalled sneaking into his parents' bedroom and taking loose change from his father's bureau to buy more "fixes."

When I first met Martin, he was depressed and lonely. Whenever he was around others, he covered his pain, and later, when he was alone, he buried his feelings deeper and deeper with sugar, simple carbohydrates, salt and fat. He was a telemarketer by trade, and although he sat day after day in a room packed with others, he never got to know any of his fellow coworkers. Each person was always on the phone. Lunches and breaks were strictly regulated, and there was never time to talk.

Martin came to see me regularly for about three years. During that time, he built trust in me (and Sapphi) and began to seek other connection opportunities. He found a support group not too far from his home and slowly began building relationships there. He found others interested in the same things he enjoyed and began going to movies, plays, and museums with other people. He started exercising and joined a local "judgment-free-zone" gym. He also attended a program for people who wanted to lose weight.

As his health improved and his connections grew, Martin was no longer the sad, isolated man I had met years earlier. He volunteered at the SPCA walking dogs and eventually adopted a little puppy to keep him company at home. Martin began to realize that although he was different from his father and brothers, and had been the recipient of family scorn and victim of hurtful jokes, he was not "bad" or "weird" or "wrong." He was fine the way he was, and as he accepted that more and more, his life continued to improve.

The last time I saw Martin he was doing well. He reported that he was still fearful of dating, but as he continued growing closer to people, he could imagine having a viable relationship in the future. He and his puppy were happily living a very different life than Martin had ever known. He promised to call if he ever wanted to meet again, but I doubt I will hear from him. He was rapidly moving in a positive direction.

Jane – who came from a long line of problem eaters

W e learn how to behave in the world by observing our parents, who learned by watching their parents. Jane's mother had a mother who had a mother who…. In Jane's family, all the women as far back as Jane could trace had difficulty accepting their bodies. As a matter of fact, every one of them had experienced major problems feeding themselves and maintaining a healthy weight. Jane's mother was no exception. She had been trained by her mother, who had been trained by her mother, and so on. Well, you get the idea.

When Jane was born in 1948, conventions of the time dictated that babies be fed on a time schedule whether they were hungry or not. Jane received regular feedings by the clock but never really developed the ability to recognize hunger. She had no idea what it felt like to be physically ready to eat. She did, however, know whether or not it was time to eat. Her mother was doing the best she could for Jane and didn't want her daughter to grow up perpetuating the eating and body image problems that had plagued her family for generations. As it turns out, though, her mother's anxiety about doing this created the exact problems that she was trying to help Jane avoid. Jane became increasingly anxious, biting her fingernails to the quick and wetting her bed until age fourteen.

Jane remembered that each day revolved around food—how much to have, how little, and how often. Her mother watched her vigilantly, and Jane felt she could never just relax and enjoy her food. She saw her mother measure servings and add up lists of calorie counts. She remembered watching Jack LaLane on television and her mother making attempts now and then to exercise along with him. She thought it was fun at first to do the exercises with her mother, but when it was strongly suggested that she exercise more, she balked at the idea.

Jane's family lived in the suburbs. Her father was an electrician, and her mother was a stay-at-home mom who had a hair salon in their home for many years. She had three other siblings—a sister and two brothers. Jane's mother carefully watched both of her daughters, but Jane felt she was specifically targeted as her mother's "project." She felt she was watched constantly, and even the slightest extra bite of food resulted in guilt and shame. Eventually, this happened whether her mother was nearby or not.

The cycle of deprivation followed by overeating, followed by shame and guilt, followed by more overeating had begun. Jane's life became more and more wrapped up in concerns about her eating habits, her weight, and her appearance. When she was about twelve years old, Jane recalled her mother taking her to a weight-loss group that she attended to help her daughter with her problem. Jane was weighed and told she had thirteen pounds to lose. This was a confusing experience. She loved her mother for caring about her and simultaneously loathed her for it. This little girl who was really not overweight, as proven by photographs taken of her at that time, was made to feel inferior, inadequate, and defective.

Like so many of us, Jane turned to sugar, simple carbohydrates, salt and fat for solace. She knew a sugar and simple carbohydrate fix would help her cope with life. She ate bags of potato chips and candy in secret and, at times, even stole money from her mother's change purse to purchase a quick fix at the corner store on the way to or from school. This added enormously to her shame and guilt. Her self-image was badly damaged, and despite her excellent grades and her accomplishments as a musician, her self-esteem plummeted. Jane was also aware of the messages she was receiving outside of her home.

She saw images of anorexic models in magazines and on television. She noticed other women's body sizes, constantly comparing herself to each one and always finding she came up short. Everywhere she turned, she received messages that confirmed her inadequacy. She had no idea how the family dynamics and social factors were impacting her self-perception. She assumed something was very wrong with her and spent each day trying to conceal her flaws from others, while feeling that her weight, which was impossible to hide, betrayed her. She imagined that everyone was judging her. Her life was unbearably tense and difficult.

Until she called me for her first appointment, Jane's life was a cycle of one deprivation diet after another, each followed by periods of overeating and weight gain. The numbers kept rising on her bathroom scale, and the harder she tried to stop the self-destructive behavior, the more weight she gained. At her first appointment, she reported that she felt defeated and no longer had the energy to fight the problem.

Jane came to realize that she would only stop eating and hurting herself when she stopped fighting with herself. It seems counterintuitive to say that, but giving up the fight frees up the energy needed to begin taking care of oneself. In order to heal and move forward, Jane needed a basic understanding of her past and had to come to the realization that she was not to blame for the problems she was having with food control, body image, and self-esteem. These behaviors were shaped early in her life, and she had been doing everything she could to solve the problem of her eating and her expanding waistline.

Once she was able to realize the dynamics that had led her into this maze of yo-yo diets and unhealthy starvation attempts, she was able to put together a plan. It took months of baby steps—three steps forward, one step back—but eventually, she crafted a healthy lifestyle. Now Jane feels better about herself. She eats well and exercises several times a week. She has formed a small support group of female friends who get together to have fun and bear witness to each other's lives. They talk, laugh, and cry together. The group members have much in common with Jane. Many are mothers themselves and are helping each other to break the cycle of mothers passing their food-control and body image issues down to their daughters, granddaughters, and great-granddaughters.

The last time I heard from Jane she was doing well and reported that on most days, not every day, she felt energized and positive. She still wished her extra pounds would simply vanish but reminded herself that her weight loss would be more permanent if it was slow and steady. She now has a daughter and is doing her best to impart healthy values about nutrition, exercise, and general self-care. She sounded happy, and that was the primary goal!

Susie – who became the caretaker in the face of alcohol abuse in her family

Susie grew up in a large family in a small Midwestern town. She was the oldest of twelve brothers and sisters. Her parents operated a small farm, growing vegetables and collecting eggs, but could barely scratch out a living from all their hard labor. Susie recalled meals of broth and, if they were lucky, peanut butter on a slice of white bread. She also remembered having to work hard every day. One of her brothers was older than the rest of her younger siblings, but he wasn't much help to her. The boys were herded outside to help with farm chores, and the girls were kept indoors to attend to domestic tasks. Since Susie was the eldest, the bulk of the household chores fell on her shoulders.

She said her father worked hard all day, but around five o'clock, he would start his nightly drinking ritual. He favored hard liquor, and every night he treated himself to a number of strong drinks. After his drinking began in the evening, Susie watched carefully to see what kind of a mood followed each sip. Sometimes he would become agitated and volatile, while at other times he would be melancholy and sentimental. Susie never knew which personality would show up at the supper table. The atmosphere was tense, and eating was not pleasurable; instead, it was a time she dreaded.

Because there were so many younger children in the family, Susie fell into a caretaker role at a very young age. She remembered her mother being pregnant most of the time and unable to manage her demanding tasks. Susie stepped into her mothering role easily and felt she had actually raised her eleven younger siblings while her mother slept and her father drank. She felt proud of herself and was praised for being such a good helper, but at the same time, she could feel anxiety and rage mounting inside.

This caretaking behavior followed Susie throughout her life. She reported that she never felt happy—always working harder to take care of everyone around her in an attempt to finally feel OK. This way of connecting with others was not satisfying, and although there was never an abundance of food available, Susie built a huge wall of resentment, which she fortified with anything she could find to eat—mostly sugar and white flour products with occasional store-bought cupcakes and jelly donuts. She reported that she had two states of being—either overly busy or eating to dull the pain that would sneak up on her whenever she took a moment to rest.

It is easy to understand why Susie felt compelled to hide her sadness and frustration in a sugar, simple carbohydrates, salt and fats habit. She was busy from early morning until late at night. Even if she had a few minutes of spare time, the farm where her family lived was isolated—many miles from the next property. She had no friends, no confidants, and no support system. Sugary, fatty foods filled the void. As we know, these foods will do this quite effectively for a while. Sugar alone is a powerful emotion soother. Combined with fat, it is even more compelling. Add salt and you have the perfect anesthetic mix. It works! It dulls your emotions and soothes difficult feelings. It only does this for a short time, however, and soon it is time for another "fix" to take the edge off.

As Susie matured and moved into adulthood, she badly wanted to leave farm life behind. This was difficult for her because she felt she was abandoning her younger siblings, who were like her own children. She knew it would not be healthy for her to remain on the farm, but she had no idea where to go or how to cope with the world outside her home.

She attended the local high school, and there she met a boy named Kevin. Susie was nineteen when she got pregnant and then had an excuse to leave home to make her own home with Kevin. They were both young, and the marriage didn't last. After their daughter was born, Kevin began drinking, and Susie found the courage to leave the relationship. She worked hard, found a waitress job, and single-parented her little girl. Eventually, she met and married a nice, gentle man who loved her very much. She loved him, but she still felt helpless to stop her self-destructive eating behaviors.

By the time she entered therapy, she was very unhealthy and at an extremely high, dangerous weight. Her doctor had just diagnosed her with type 2 diabetes, and she was heartbroken and discouraged. It took quite a long time for Susie to put the pieces of her past together and forgive herself for her weight gain. Once she realized how much love and care she had always generously given others, she began to give herself a little of the love and care she deserved. Today she is doing well working as a secretary in a large firm and enjoying her family. The weight is coming off one ounce at a time, one pound at a time.

There are days when she again finds herself helplessly in the midst of a negative spin, but she now has the skills to alter her self-destructive course. She knows how to renew her efforts to make self-care her number one priority, and that this is a lifelong process. Overall, she was taking very good care of herself and finding much joy both at work and at home when we parted.

Paula – who yearned for approval

Paula learned as a child that her life was good if she received approval and unpleasant when she didn't. Approval was the key in her family. If her mother disapproved of something Paula said or did, she was harshly criticized and often humiliated. She remembered many occasions when she was belittled in front of others. She would flood with shame and wished she could disappear. Every day was a test. If she said or did something wrong, she was punished. If she said and did what she thought was OK, she could still be wrong and still be punished. The game was confusing. It never made sense. Paula remembered always being on edge, waiting to see how she would be received. Riddled with anxiety, she was always on guard, even when she didn't know what she was on guard against.

Paula's mother was a single parent, and Paula never knew her father. Her mother told her he was a useless man who didn't care about her or Paula. He proved this by leaving when Paula was only two years old. According to Paula's memory, her mother always implied she was the reason her father had left. Because of this, Paula was convinced something must be terribly wrong with her, that she must be "bad." There was no one to tell her anything different. She had no extended family, and her mother never entertained or had friends drop by.

Paula's mother worked as a saleswoman in a local department store. Her hours were often long, and she would come home at night complaining of aching feet and the poor pay she received. She was always exhausted and crabby. Since Paula was an only child, she was the sole recipient of her mother's discontent. She tried as hard as she could to please her mother and take care of her. Paula only felt safe when she was getting her mother's approval for waiting on her hand and foot. If she could keep showing her mother that she was a good daughter by being subservient and cheerful and getting good grades, then it would surely prove she was a lovable person and that her father had not abandoned them by any fault of hers.

It was confusing business, and soon Paula lost her sense of self. She focused on escaping her mother's ridicule by trying to please this woman who was so often abusive. This behavior eventually spread to Paula's other relationships, and it wasn't long before she made the decision that her life should be devoted to serving others and avoiding conflict at all cost. Paula was unhappy and remembered sitting alone in her living room, curled up on the end of the sofa, wishing her life were different. She longed for brothers and sisters. She dreamed of having a puppy. She had asked her mother for a dog a number of times, but her mother refused to get one, saying it would be too expensive to feed. She told Paula how stupid and ridiculous she was to even think of it. This type of remark from her mother always led Paula to think harder of ways she could make her mother happier.

Paula wished for more money for her and her mom. She thought her mother might love her more if she didn't have to work such long, tiring hours, but secretly, she knew better. Sometimes she even found herself wishing for a different mother. This thought would always precipitate a deluge of guilt and shame, and then Paula would berate herself. What little self-esteem, she had was repeatedly damaged. She maintained good grades in school, but she felt terrible about herself. Things always seemed to go from bad to worse and then to even worse.

Many of the kids made fun of her at school. She never had the right clothes or said or did the right things. She became quiet, only joining in when she could help someone else. The others eventually caught on to Paula's benevolent personality, and she became the go-to person whenever they wanted something. She began doing favors for her classmates, and because she was very bright and her grades were excellent, she even did homework for a few of them. Paula got attention from her "friends" because of her service to them, and she mistook this attention for friendship. She felt lost if nothing was asked of her. She isolated herself, and weekends were long and lonely. Paula was sad. She couldn't put her finger on why. The life she had was the only one she knew, and she continued to believe something was wrong with her.

When Paula was a senior in high school, her mother died. She was seventeen. Her mother had a heart attack, and Paula discovered her body in bed when her mother failed to get up for work. At first, Paula described feeling lost and blamed herself for her mother's death. She was placed in a foster home with a loving family and began psychotherapy sessions. For many months, Paula wouldn't speak to the therapist. She was too ashamed, too scared, and still convinced she was "bad."

The foster family helped Paula gain admission to a nearby college, and gradually, she began making friends. She recalled one special friend named Dotty who confronted her one day. She asked Paula why she was always doing things to help everybody else. Dotty pointed out that although she knew Paula meant well, it was annoying at times. Initially, Paula felt hurt but soon realized Dotty was a true friend who was sincerely interested in her well-being. Paula began to question her own behavior, and little by little she began to relax—at least a little.

When Paula appeared in my office, she was twenty-two years old and desperately trying to figure out why she was unhappy so much of the time. She had been eating compulsively for as long as she could remember. She wasn't exercising at all, and her health was poor. She looked pale, tired, and far older than twenty-two.

It took a while for Paula to understand the impact her past had upon her. She was tired of being a "human doing" instead of a "human being." She had a notion that her constant caretaking was inappropriate and that this behavior was self-harming. It was a wonderful moment in therapy when Paula realized that it was OK for her to stop, slow down, and turn her focus of attention inward—truly an aha moment. Starved for love, she knew deep inside she was using pastries and pasta to cover her hurt, anger, and sadness.

Paula began the arduous task of putting the pieces of her life together. She spent time relating the facts of her childhood and growing up with a frustrated, abusive mother. Then she switched the focus of her attention to the present and talked about how she wished to live her life now, in the present. She learned some basic communication and assertiveness skills, and her social network expanded. To her amazement, Paula discovered that friends seemed to like her more when she did less for them. It was hard for her to imagine they might just like her because she was sincerely likable. These positive messages slipped into her belief system as well as extended the limits of her thinking.

The last time I saw Paula she had been dating a lovely man for about a year. At her final session, she brought him with her to meet me. He seemed kind and loving, and they planned to marry and move to another state. His employer was transferring him to a new position in his company, which meant more money, among other benefits. Paula beamed as she introduced her fiancé. I will never forget how relaxed and peaceful they seemed together. As they left the office, she turned, winked happily, and said, "The first thing we're going to do when we get settled is shop for a puppy!"

Paula knows she can always call me if she wants or needs to. I am fairly sure I won't hear from her. She planned to find a therapist in her new area to continue the fine work she was doing. She had begun exercising and eating well, she was resting and relaxing more, and as far as I know, she is enjoying her journey and creating her delicious life at last. I picture her joyfully walking along with her husband and a frisky little bouncy puppy.

Mike – the overachiever

M ike sounded frightened when he made an appointment. He told me he wanted to straighten some things out about his life and that lately he had been having trouble controlling his anger. His wife was threatening to leave him, and he felt desperate, so we scheduled time for him to come in that afternoon.

One look at Mike told me he had not slept or taken care of himself for quite a while. He was nervous, tired, and stressed. He relaxed a bit as he began to tell me his story. Mike had been married for eight years when his wife, Ellen, told him she was unhappy and wanted a separation. Mike was against it and was confused about Ellen's reasoning. He told her he did not understand, but all she would say was that she was unhappy. The couple had two children—a six-year-old boy and a seven-year-old girl. He said both children seemed to be doing well at that time, but he worried the children would suffer if he and Ellen separated.

Mike was from a small family. He had only one brother, who was two years older. His mother was a high school teacher, and his father was a dentist. Both he and his brother had excelled in school and sports, and much was expected of them, especially Mike who, although younger, "set the bar" for the two boys. Mike's brother completed high school and, against both parents' wishes, joined the Marines. Mike, on the other hand, felt it was up to him to carry on family traditions and went straight to a prestigious college after high school graduation. He wanted to study courses that would set him on the right path for medical school.

Mike soon excelled in all his classes and maintained a high grade point average throughout college. He was a noted athlete, captain of the football team, and popular with his peers. He remembered college life as stressful, and although he had fun, he felt pressured to achieve top grades and make his father proud. He worked hard and played hard, but soon it became too much.

Mike joined a fraternity that was known on campus as a "party house." He thought if he partied a little more, he could better manage the pressures of college life. It didn't take him long to establish a significant relationship with the house beer keg, and in time, both his grades and health began to suffer. Mike sought the services of a counselor and realized he had a significant problem with alcohol. He vowed to give up drinking and moved out of the fraternity house.

At the time, he had been dating Ellen for two months, and she invited him to move in with her. He took her up on her offer, and the pair settled in together. Mike had little difficulty giving up alcohol but soon replaced that addiction with another—food.

Mike and Ellen got engaged and planned the wedding date for a year after graduation; however, Ellen's unexpected pregnancy forced them to push up the date. Their baby entered the world when Mike was halfway through his junior year. Ellen left school to care for their daughter. A year later, they added a son to the family. Pressures mounted, and Mike struggled to keep up with his finances, family, and academic responsibilities.

To "take the edge off," Mike began to eat more. He was not aware that foods containing sugar, simple carbohydrates, salt and fat were highly addictive for a lot of people. These foods raise the beta-endorphins in our brain and anesthetize our feelings. They serve as a most effective buffer, protecting us from difficult emotions, and Mike quickly learned that a cupcake or big bowl of pasta could calm him down and replace his pain with momentary pleasure. This worked well at first, but soon he began to gain weight and experienced increased exhaustion. He couldn't sleep and was nervous and depressed. He was no longer the "star," and his grades went down as the numbers on the scale went up. He became more and more frustrated, out of control, and angry.

By the time I met Mike, he admittedly felt his life was a total failure. He had not been able to pursue the medical career he had planned and never attended graduate school of any kind. He had a lucrative job in a real estate office but did not find it satisfying. He felt his job was a dead end and saw no future opportunities for advancement. He felt trapped and dependent on sugar and was furious about the whole picture. His life was falling apart around him, and his angry outbursts were impossible to control. Mike needed help. He really wanted to keep his marriage and family intact.

I asked Mike to bring Ellen to his next appointment, and the three of us talked about Mike's addiction and why his present anger made sense. The pressure on him to excel since childhood had created a burden that drove Mike first to alcohol and then to comfort food. We all agreed his behavior needed to change, and the couple made a "no leave for three months" agreement.

During the next three months, Mike faithfully came to every appointment. We focused on his unrealistic self-expectations and on identifying some things—other than eating—he could do to cope with his frustration. The more Mike talked, the more he relaxed and began having some fun. He and Ellen set one night a week for a "date" and began getting to know each other all over again. Mike started running and went to the local YMCA three times a week to weight train. He changed his eating habits and stopped filling his belly with sugar, simple carbohydrates, salt and fat. His energy level rose, and his mood stabilized.

He and Ellen began working as a team. They shared the task of cooking meals. She went back to school part time, and Mike started spending more time with his children. He explored other career options, and last I knew, he was considering several online programs. He was feeling well, his life was coming into balance, and he was more joyful every day.

Ultimately, the three-month deadline came and went, and Mike and Ellen said they felt closer than ever.

Jill – who tried to fit into a passive, caretaker role

Jill presented herself at my office stating she had always been overweight and felt helpless to change. She was discouraged. She had tried every diet she knew of and some even I had not heard of. Jill was experiencing health problems caused by her excess pounds. She was frightened and had given up on herself. She said she could not imagine change but hoped I could make her better. She remarked, "I hope this will fix me." Her self-esteem was dreadfully low, and she seemed tired and listless.

Jill had been overweight all her life. Her mother was overweight, as were her grandmothers. Her father was a laborer who drank beer every night while watching TV. He, too, was well over the obesity mark. Jill's sister also struggled with food control, and all the women in the house had tried diet after diet to no avail. Jill recalled being teased for her size by the other children at school and realized she had always isolated herself.

She viewed all of the women in her family as passive, and although her dad was either absent from home or sitting on the couch and drinking, it was clear that he was the boss. Jill's mother waited on him hand and foot. He was always served his meals on time, and she prepared only what he wanted. She catered to him and was always at his service, even when Jill felt his needs seemed unreasonable.

What had Jill learned by witnessing her mother's behavior? How could she have grown into a clear and assertive woman with no role models to follow? Jill's mother soothed herself with food, and Jill was happy to follow suit. Her mother bought candy and pastries and sometimes made huge batches of pasta with meatballs and sauce. Jill and her sister would join their mother in the evening for late-night snacks of sweets, pasta, chips, or big bowls of ice cream. These foods helped the three women feel better and calmer and allowed them to continue to be passive. The sugar fix was temporary, however, and the numbers on the scale continued to rise for Jill and everyone else in the family.

It wasn't long before Jill's life consisted entirely of meals followed by snacks, followed by the next meal. She was tired and reported getting winded on the stairs even in grammar school. She led a sedentary life watching television, napping, or reading romance novels. She had little interest in outside activities and had no friends throughout grammar school and high school.

After high school, Jill wanted to stay at home, but her parents told her she either had to enroll in some type of further schooling or find a job. She was not going to spend the rest of her life sitting on their couch, eating their food, and not contributing to the household. Jill chose to look for work and began perusing websites that posted jobs. She had no experience and began applying for menial work. She was able to schedule a few interviews, but she did not interview well and was unsuccessful in landing a position anywhere.

Jill felt sure she had been rejected because of her appearance. She was not able to prove this, of course, because no one said they were passing her up for that reason. They always cited other reasons, such as her lack of experience, or they would take one look at her and tell her the position she was applying for had already been filled. This chain of rejections replicated Jill's personal history of rejections, and her self-esteem was as low as it could get.

She remembered feeling suicidal and said she would have attempted suicide if she wasn't so scared. She became severely depressed and refused to leave her bedroom for several weeks. Jill's parents and her sister tried to lift her spirits and motivate her to do something to no avail. So Jill just "checked out." She slept and ate and continued to feel worse each day.

Eventually, Jill realized that she could not continue to eat, lie around, and do nothing. There was a part of her that wanted to make something of her life. She began a search for a healthy way to make changes, and her medical doctor suggested therapy. By the time Jill entered my office, she was so sufficiently motivated by her intense pain that she was open to suggestion.

She joined an organization for overeaters and learned she was not alone. She began making important, healthy changes. Her mother and sister were thrilled and decided to attend meetings with her. At first, they went under the pretense they were helping Jill, but soon realized they needed help as much as she did. Soon all three women were supporting each other in creating healthier bodies through dietary changes and a small amount of exercise.

Jill met others in this group who shared her lifelong struggle with weight management. She asked a woman she admired to be her sponsor, and she spoke to this woman every morning to discuss what foods she would choose that day and to get encouragement and support. Jill faithfully attended meetings at least five times per week and soon began to shed some of the stubborn pounds she had been hanging on to all her life.

As Jill continued her quest for radiant health and increased energy, she became more assertive, and her self-image gradually improved. She started making friends, and her social connections became extremely valuable and central in her life. She no longer felt powerless and victimized. She did remarkable work in her therapy sessions and reversed her old self-defeating behaviors. She met Nancy at a dinner party, and they became confidants and best friends. They spent a lot of time together and began to fall in love.

When Jill terminated her treatment, she and Nancy were dating, and she was really enjoying the fun life was offering her. I haven't heard from her in over two years now, but I trust she is doing well. She knows she can always contact me if she wishes, but we agreed that no news was good news.

Mia – who learned that being overweight was an advantage

Mia learned early in her life that extra weight could actually give her an advantage. In her large extended family, her grandmother was clearly the matriarch, and Mia noticed that this large woman was treated with reverence, respect, and some fear. Mia associated her grandmother's large size with power and wanted to be like this woman she revered. She observed that all of the females in her large family grouping were obese, and the men, most of whom were not overweight, deferred to the women in matters of importance. So Mia deduced that size mattered in a positive way. She explained to me that she had grown up with the clear message that in order to be a successful and powerful woman, one also had to be large.

Both she and her sister never refused pastries, sweets, and pasta. It never occurred to her to say no. These foods were staples in her home, and everyone ate their fill. Mia was out of touch with her physical appetite and ate all the sugar and fat she could. She was extremely addicted, and no one cared or noticed. All the women in the family were in the same boat.

When Mia went to grammar school, and later high school, she was often the brunt of other students' cruel jokes about her size, her clothes, and her family. Mia recalled one day when three girls began taunting her in the hall, and she ducked into the nearest girls' bathroom to escape. The girls followed her inside to continue their verbal abuse. Mia told them she'd had enough and surprised herself by lunging at the girl she thought was the leader of the pack. She and her opponent tumbled to the floor, hitting one another and pulling each other's hair. She remembered with horror seeing blood on the face of the other girl.

The next memory Mia had of the event was being taken to the principal's office and subsequently being sent home for the remainder of the day. She sat in the office for quite a while in her soiled and torn clothes. The other girl never came into the principal's office, and Mia later learned she had been taken to the nurse's office and then to the hospital emergency room, where she was evaluated for internal injuries. There were none, and the girl was allowed back to school the next day.

When Mia's mother arrived at the school to pick her up, she angrily marched Mia down the corridor while other students watched her pass. She felt humiliated, but at the same time, triumphant. This was the first time she found the strength and courage to fight back, and in her mind, she had won the altercation hands down.

No one teased Mia anymore following that fateful day. A few girls expressed admiration for her, and for the first time, she made some friends. This reinforced her belief that being overweight was an advantage. Mia soon noticed that in addition to strength and power, being overweight had other benefits as well. She used her weight as an excuse to skip gym class and avoid dances and parties. She was unconsciously using her size and stature to keep herself safe from ridicule and rejection. It gave her a reason to continue her lifestyle of cakes and big bowls of ice cream with chocolate sauce, whipped cream, nuts, and of course, a cherry (or two or three) on top.

By the time Mia came to see me at age thirty-one, she was suffering from a number of weight-related health issues. She had joint problems, and her cardiologist had issued severe warnings about the condition of her heart. Her primary care physician diagnosed her with type 2 diabetes, and Mia was afraid to continue her self-abusive behavior. She described feeling frightened, hopeless, and depressed.

Mia faced a conundrum that many women have had to conquer. If she lost weight, she would be healthier, but would she be happier? This was a topic of a number of our sessions, because as she became healthier, she would simultaneously distance herself from other family females who were not taking steps to improve their own health. This could be a major barrier to her progress if not fully understood and resolved.

If all were eating bowls of ice cream and she refused to join them, she was afraid they would disapprove of her and isolate her from the family. Family ties were of primary importance to her, and her fear of abandonment battled with her desire to be healthy. We spent quite a few sessions discussing this issue, and eventually, Mia was able to talk with her mother and sister about her fear. They assured her they would love her no matter what she weighed, and only with that reassurance could Mia tentatively move forward.

Because of Mia's ill health, she was motivated by fear. This helped her to start, but to be successful, she needed to turn her focus inward and begin to appreciate herself. It took Mia a long time to develop some empathy for herself and look at weight loss as a positive movement forward instead of a betrayal of her loved ones.

Once Mia was able to relate some of her history to me and understand why she had been eating so voraciously all of her life, she was able to stop bingeing and beating herself up. She realized there were valid reasons for her weight that were no longer important. Together, we were able to chart a course toward health and joyful living. This was not easy for Mia, but she was determined to help herself and gradually made herself her number one priority. The last time we met she was well on her way to radiant health and her joyful, delicious life.

Sally – who preferred the illusion of safety at home

S ally contacted me to make an appointment and was tearful on the phone, speaking in a faltering, quiet voice. She told me her husband had left her and filed for divorce and that she didn't know what to do. I asked her to come in as soon as she could, and we met early that evening. When she arrived, Sally was extremely anxious and had great difficulty making eye contact. She whimpered, and sadly related the events of the past few days.

Her husband had seemed unhappy for a long time, but he had recently become more distant than ever. They no longer did things together or talked as they had at the start of their relationship. They lost the connection she remembered they had when they first met. The marriage she thought was going to last forever appeared to be over after only three years. Sally said that although her husband frequently seemed discontent, she was shocked when he announced he was leaving her. The couple had no children and both worked, so her husband told her the divorce would be quick and simple. Sally was both confused and devastated. She didn't feel she could return to her secretarial job because she had been unable to sleep all week and couldn't concentrate.

I encouraged Sally to make an emergency appointment with her physician to discuss the possibility of getting a small amount of medication to lower her anxiety during this crisis and help her get some badly needed rest. She agreed to do this as soon as she got home, and we made a plan for her to come back three days later and to call me in the meantime if she was in crisis. I also asked her if she had a support system, and she said she there was one person whom she considered a friend, a woman she worked with named Nicki. She promised to call Nicki, explain her circumstances, and talk with her about her situation and her feelings.

I told Sally our time was up, and she walked reluctantly toward the office door with her drooping shoulders. With one hand on the doorknob, she turned to me and said, "I am pretty sure he's leaving me because I'm fat. If only I hadn't gained this weight I know he would still love me." I assured her that was most likely not the case, but we would talk more about that first thing at our next meeting.

When Sally and I met three days later, she was feeling a little better. She had asked for a few days off from work, had seen her physician, and received prescriptions for a mild antianxiety medication and a five nights' supply of sleeping pills. Because she felt her weight was the primary factor in her husband's departure, it was the first item on our agenda. I explained that in order to make sense of her failing marriage and what was going on in the present, I wanted to talk briefly about her history. She was agreeable, and I asked her to tell me something about her family.

Sally was an only child who grew up in New York City. She and her parents lived in what she described as a large, beautiful apartment close to the park and to the bank where her father worked. The family was affluent, and finances were never an issue. Sally's parents enrolled her in the best private schools, and she earned above average grades throughout grammar and high school. Following graduation, she enrolled in a secretarial college in Connecticut but left after only one semester because she didn't enjoy dorm living and being away from the safety of home. She described herself as a bookworm who never went outdoors. Her world became more and more narrow, and she said she spent her days reading and watching TV with her mother.

Sally recalled being twenty years old when her parents invited some of her father's colleagues to their apartment for dinner and she met Chuck, who later became her husband. When they first talked, she remembered being nervous and shy. He began inviting her out on dates to the movies and dinner, and gradually, she found herself falling in love. Eventually, she developed enough trust in him to agree to his marriage proposal. They had a small wedding in New York City, with only their immediate families in attendance. At first, their marriage was happy, and she felt comfortable living away from her parents.

After a short time, Chuck became impatient with Sally when she refused to leave their home. She resisted his efforts to interest her in outside activities and declined any invitations to go out with friends. Sally preferred to remain at home and read, watch TV, and of course, eat as she had growing up.

When I questioned her further about her early years, she recalled that her mother was always nearby. Sally's mother had lost a child before she was born. It was a death known at the time as "crib death"; therefore, her mother was afraid of losing Sally as well. She was extremely overprotective, and Sally remembered her mother would never let her out of her sight. She was constantly warned of the dangers everywhere. If she went outside without a hat, she was told she could catch her death of cold. If she held a pair of scissors in her hand, she might cut herself and have to be rushed to the hospital. If she wanted to step outside, something bad would surely happen to her. Every activity, from roller-skating to playing with friends to riding a bicycle, was said to be far too hazardous for Sally to consider. She soon learned the world was, indeed, a dangerous place. Her anxiety grew because she always felt just a breath away from harm. It was logical that she would eat to soothe her anxiety and stay indoors next to her mother, the television, and a plate of gooey chocolate chip cookies. The routine helped her feel safe.

As we explored Sally's learned helplessness and her unfounded fears, she began to recognize the connection between the events of her childhood and her failure to relax and enjoy her life in the present. Chuck did divorce her. He had already moved on and was involved with another woman. Sally was terribly sad about this and went through an intense grieving process. She continued her sessions with me, however, and gradually, she ventured out into the world one small step at a time.

She enrolled in an assertiveness class at her local college and joined a divorcee support group. People at work expressed their concern and began asking her to join them for social gatherings after work and on weekends. She became more adventurous and soon was able to invite friends to visit her apartment or go out to movies or dinners. After three months, she joined an art class and was excited to share some of her paintings with me. She was quite talented, and her watercolor flowers were bright and cheerful. She also started exercising. At first, she walked a few minutes a day and later joined the neighborhood gym for full workouts. Each step she took on her own behalf strengthened her resolve to create a life of balance and joy.

Sally learned that her fears had been imposed upon her at a very early age and that she no longer needed to hide away in a self-imposed sugar-coated prison. She appreciated that her parents, particularly her mother, had meant well by protecting her but also understood her mother's overprotection had not been helpful and had inhibited her ability to enjoy a rich and rewarding life. She learned it was all right to appreciate and forgive her mother, while at the same time allowing herself to experience anger that her life had unfolded in this way.

Sally became more confident as she continued to explore the world around her. Her self-esteem and body image improved, and her weight stabilized at a healthy number on the scale. When I last saw her she was managing her life quite well. She had made many friends and was involved in a number of activities she enjoyed. She promised to call if she started isolating and overeating again, but it has been two years so far, and I haven't heard from her.

A Summary

If you read the stories, were you able to identify similarities and differences between yourself and some of the people in the case studies? Most likely, you could find a few things that matched your experiences and feelings, while others may not have resonated with you. We are all different, but at the same time, we have much in common. I have noticed a number of common factors shared by many of the women who have come to see me during the twenty-five years of my practice, which I have listed below for you. Whether you read the stories or not, see how many of these factors align with parts of your experience.

COMMON HISTORICAL FACTORS:

<u>Women feel invalidated.</u>

Women often report feeling invalidated during their lifetimes. When they attempted to tell their parents, teachers or friends how they felt, they were sometimes ignored and often told they shouldn't feel that way. This frustrating and painful experience led many women to keep their true feelings to themselves. Instead of being encouraged to express their authentic emotions, they were told to feel what others wanted them to feel. In this way, many women grew out of touch with their own emotions and eventually sought validation and approval by thinking and feeling what they expected they "should" be thinking and feeling, rather than what they actually were experiencing.

Because our feelings are our internal guidance system, it is imperative that we learn to recognize and express our genuine emotions. I will discuss this in more detail later in the book. For now, it is important to realize that your feelings, whatever they may be, are valid. At first, it may be difficult for many of you to trust your emotions if you have spent years denying your true feelings to gain approval and avoid invalidation. It is well worth the effort to tune in to your feelings and learn to express yourself.

Only when you feel authentic and clear will you be able to move toward health, freedom, and joy. Once you can express yourself openly and assert your right to do so, you will be able to take charge of your life, and your weight issues will fade into the background.

<u>Women cannot make sense of a "crazy-making" world.</u>

Frequently, women tell me that they felt confused by the culture in their home. They received mixed messages and had trouble making sense of the world around them. You may have heard the expression "There's an elephant in the room." This means many issues in a family, which may seem obvious to a young person, are never acknowledged or addressed. The child or teen observes people pretending that all is fine, while underneath the facade, things are not fine at all. People hold their thoughts and feelings inside and cannot relate honestly or authentically with each other. Children sense this but usually end up thinking that something is wrong with them for experiencing the world so differently from the way others *appear* to be experiencing it.

This is a common element in many families. Parents may not know how to confront difficult situations and may lack the communication skills necessary to do so. They may be held back by fear (of upsetting someone else, incurring another's anger, being abandoned, or being invalidated once again). Family members play the roles they have been assigned in the family and act as they imagine they are supposed to, but all the while feel confused, helpless, and weak.

This breeds self-doubt and confusion. It is hard to feel confident and good about yourself when the world around you is not making sense. It is easier to play along and eat to dull your feelings than to risk disrupting the family system.

<u>Women think they aren't good enough.</u>

Women are constantly bombarded with messages about how to look, how to act, what to say, and so on. Messages come from all directions—from family, friends, institutions, and the media. Women are constantly being looked at and evaluated. Their weight seems to be everyone's business, and well-meaning relatives may offer advice about ways to be more slender and attractive. This is a dreadful predicament for any woman.

If you pause in the supermarket checkout line, you will find it difficult (and often impossible) to spot a publication that won't tell you what and how you need to change. Headlines advertise ways to flatten your tummy, tighten your buttocks, get rid of your unsightly bulges, perform better in bed, and get rid of acne. You can buy these magazines and learn how to have a smoother, fresher complexion, reduce wrinkles, and lift your sagging breasts, all the while preparing and serving amazing meals in minutes. You will read about the importance of diet and exercise and most likely unearth much conflicting information. If you try to follow all of the advice dispensed from the newsstand, you will likely become more discouraged and eat even more to soothe the painful feelings you will experience realizing that you can't do or have it all.

Along with these headlines, you will find slender smiling women who are held up as examples of how we all should look. These photographs are often altered, with blemishes (and even pores) airbrushed away. Breasts are enlarged, waistlines diminished, eyelashes lengthened, and legs sculpted. We can't really tell what's real and what isn't, but we are sure we don't look like that.

Is it any wonder that women have a hard time maintaining a positive body image and a healthy level of self-esteem?

<u>Women try in vain to be perfect.</u>

In my role as a professional speaker, I have the opportunity to address large audiences about women's issues. I joke with my audience members that there are probably no women in the room who expect themselves to be perfect. This usually prompts loud laughter as each woman looks around and realizes they are all the same. Most, if not all, women hold unrealistic expectations of themselves. They would never expect such perfection from others, but they continue to set impossibly high goals for themselves.

Setting unrealistic, impossible goals leads to failure every single time. We are all human, and although it is wise to set challenging goals, it is self-destructive to hold perfection as the only acceptable outcome. If we continually set ourselves up to fail, we can never feel good about ourselves. Instead, we become discouraged and see ourselves as failures. This leads to self-punishment and often to the bakery or candy aisle. Then we eat to soothe ourselves and suppress painful emotions.

Some women spend years trapped in this loop. They set themselves up to be perfect, fail, feel badly, and then eat to feel better. They resolve to perform better in the future. Since they still can't behave perfectly every minute, they set themselves up to fail again.

Then they beat themselves up, eat to feel better, end up feeling worse, and the cycle repeats itself again and again.

As you read this book, you will discover ways to end the self-destructive cycle once and for all. You do not have to continue to feel like a victim, failing to manage your life. You empower yourself to change once you understand how and why you have been harming yourself and begin making self-loving choices instead of self-harming ones.

<u>Women blame themselves for their inability to control their eating behavior.</u>

Many women come to see me stating they have no willpower and feel like failures. Often, they remark that eating is the one area in which they feel helpless and out of control. They may be successful in business and family life, but when it comes to passing up the cheesecake or potato chips, they become helpless and weak.

I do not believe in willpower. I believe women will feed themselves well when they understand the physical causes, feel good about themselves, and are able to genuinely express their emotions. Being happy, healthy, and whole and having your delicious life is not about being thin. It is about being happy with yourself at whatever size you are now. It is about self-acceptance and joy. It is about loving yourself.

It is necessary to take the focus away from feeling fat and unhappy and value the positive aspects of our lives and ourselves. It is vital to appreciate what we do have and to let go of the things that are restricting us and holding us back. Only then can we create the lives of balance and joy we so desperately want. Later in this book, we will examine ways to do so, and you will discover for yourself how to turn your former unhealthy behaviors into positive, productive ones.

Women think something is wrong with them and are outer-directed rather than inner-directed.

It is difficult, if not impossible, to feel good about ourselves when we are surrounded by evidence of our inferiority. If people are saying your feelings are wrong and you do not feel respected, valued, or heard, it is not likely that you will think you are OK. You may at first, but soon your conviction deteriorates in the face of contrary evidence. You may have noticed as you read the eleven previous stories that feeling "something is wrong with me" seems to be echoed by nearly everyone.

As children, we want to be loved and approved of. Every child deserves this, but most of us are not recipients of this unconditional love for very long, if at all. We try different behaviors, and it doesn't take long for us to figure out what behaviors bring approval and which ones bring disapproval, even punishment. We are shaped in this way by the approval (love) or withholding of approval (or love) by those around us, so we grow up looking outside of ourselves to figure out how to behave.

At some point, we are supposed to learn to think and act for ourselves, but most of us were never taught how to do so. We continue well into adulthood searching for approval, validation, and love. If we speak up, we fear abandonment, so we hold our tongues. This results in the suppression of anger, and we begin eating to keep ourselves in check. We literally stifle our feelings with sugar, simple carbohydrates, salt and fat in some form—pretzels, pasta, sweets, ice cream, or breads. We want to feel better, but we keep repeating the same behaviors and remain stuck in the same self-destructive loop.

We are bound to feel unhappy and inadequate if we can't be ourselves and be appreciated for the amazing, beautiful women we are. In the following pages, you will learn how to break out of this painful cycle once and for all. It is my sincere hope that reading this book will help you forge your own path to your delicious life of balance, radiant health and joy.

STEP II – Stop the Blame Game

Now that you have read the stories and have seen some of the ways food management problems begin, it is vital that you pull your focus from the past to the present and look toward the future. If you ruminate about the past and lament the bad experiences you have had, you will remain stuck. To be truly happy and to let go of your dependence on food, you will have to forgive and move on. I am not saying that any injustices done to you, whether purposely or inadvertently, are OK. It is never OK for a child to be abused, invalidated, or harmed in any way. But you no longer need feel like a victim.

Continuing to blame others and reflecting on the ways in which you were hurt won't help you move forward. It will hold you back and prevent you from using your energy to take care of yourself and keep your focus in the present. To create the delicious life you want, you will learn to move through painful circumstances in the present and release old, painful experiences (more about this later in "Appreciate the Pain").

What I am stressing at this point is the importance of letting go of old hurts and making a vow to be as gentle and loving with yourself as possible now. This is how you begin to feel better, look better, and make the progress you desire. Forgiving is not for the parent who abused you, the spouse who abandoned you, or the people who bullied you. Forgiveness is for you, and you alone.

All your life you have been treated unfairly, and now is the time to take the reins and create what you want in your life! You have had it! You are tired of being told what to do, how to look, and how to act. The barrage of conflicting messages you receive confuses you, and you are angry! You want to be authentic, and you want to be heard. It is no longer acceptable to diet in public and cry in private. You want real change, and the time is NOW. You are seeking radiant health and dream of a life of balance and joy. You want to feel good about yourself and recapture your zest and creativity because deep down you know that you will feel beautiful only when you make your well-being your top priority. You want to be radiant and joyful, and this book shows you how in simple, powerful, clear steps you can easily understand and adapt to your individual lifestyle.

Most of us have spent our lifetimes struggling valiantly to suppress our Appetites. We have tried diet plan after diet plan, used diet aids, exercised feverishly, all with little or no lasting success. Why do so many of us fail to lose those extra pounds? We may be very successful in other aspects of our lives, so why do we feel and act like failures in this particular area? We may feel powerful and act with purpose most of the time in most situations, but when it comes to resisting the warm rolls served with dinner or the decadent dessert, we transform into helpless, whining little children. We are not operating from a position of choice. (I choose to eat that brownie.) Instead, we go on autopilot and act from a position of helplessness. (That brownie jumped into my mouth. I couldn't help it. It's just who I am! I had nothing to do with it. I am helpless.)

What's going on? When we consider our Appetite to be tamed and have the skills necessary to click out of autopilot, why do we continue to sabotage ourselves? Deep down we know the answers. As I mentioned earlier, the diet industry is a thirteen-billion-dollar-plus industry. Much money is spent on research and marketing to convince us to swallow magic pills, purchase assorted types of weight-loss equipment, and to try various "proven" diets. These come with enticing promises of quick and easy weight loss, which will result in the vibrant health and instant self-worth we so desperately want.

We know in our hearts that these strategies will not bring us the results we are seeking. Our intuition tells us to do something different, but we do not know exactly what that is.

There is important information you must have before you can empower yourself to manage your eating. We know much more today than ever before about foods and the various ways we are affected, not only by eating them, but also by the specific ingredients manufacturers put into them to entice us and the ways these foods are marketed to us. It has been well documented that sugar, simple carbohydrates, salt and fat, particularly when combined, are highly addictive for most people. In his informative book, *The end of overeating: Taking Control of the Insatiable American Appetite*, Dr. David Kessler labels this irresistible eating experience as "hypereating," and most of us can relate to that. When most of us are faced with foods laden with sugar, simple carbohydrates, salt and fat we become helpless to stop.

Let me explain the cycle. When we eat sugar, simple carbohydrates, salt and fat, we feel good. Our feelings recede into the background, and we become immersed in the eating experience. We feel better for a short while but then crave another "fix" as the good feelings fade. We know that more sugar, simple carbohydrates, salt and fat will provide another "high," and the reward center of our brain makes us seek out this pleasure. When we are given large amounts of these foods, most of us will overeat.

For years, you may have been thinking that there was something wrong with you and that your inability to control your eating was due to a lack of willpower. We now know that that is not the case. Sugar, simple carbohydrates, salt, and fat are self-reinforcing, and we are cued to seek them out. When our desire to eat is stimulated by certain sights, sounds, or places we associate with eating, we release dopamine in our brain, and reward-seeking behavior is motivated. As Dr. Kessler points out, dopamine pushes us to seek the food we want, and we are not easily distracted from our goal; therefore, dopamine leads us to seek food. We then eat, which leads to an opioid (good feeling brain chemicals, similar to morphine or heroin) release. This stimulation of the opioid circuitry drives us to continue to eat and we then will work hard to obtain the reward of more food. In this excellent work, he goes on to expose the food industry and explains ways foods are engineered to provide exactly what we crave.

Every aspect of food manufacture and marketing is of great importance; packaging, the ambience in restaurants, noise levels, portion sizes, and even the name of the product have an effect. If we are under stress (and who isn't?), we are even hungrier and more likely to become trapped in the hypereating cycle. Dr. Kessler acknowledges that emotional learning has not traditionally been part of habit reversal but that understanding emotional eating may be the missing link necessary to stop mindless eating.

Throughout this book, you are shown ways to stop being a victim of the food industry. First, please acknowledge that your overeating behavior has not been your fault alone and has not been entirely in your control. Next, please remind yourself that this quest for health will take patience, time, and an attitude of self-acceptance and gentleness. You are given techniques for stopping this automatic eating response in its tracks and returning to balance and joy, even if you have an experience now and then of eating mindlessly and getting hooked into the victim role the food industry wants you to play. You are learning different ways to take care of yourself and how to bypass automatic responses to the food cues that abound in our culture.

You already know you want to move away from unhealthy behaviors toward healthy ones. This is critical. These goals will help you immensely as you create your own personal path away from the ploys of the food industry and toward the rewards that come with making self-loving choices as often as possible. There will be setbacks. You should know that right up front. There is no room here for absolute perfection. We can never be fully cured of conditioned hypereating, but we can listen to the important messages our feelings are communicating, treat ourselves with love and respect, and celebrate the many times we eat well, ignoring momentary lapses in judgment.

You are learning now that in addition to social causes, there are physical, emotional, and spiritual causes as well. You will have a broad understanding of this entire picture by the time you finish this book, and you will be unstoppable! You will think of food in a different way—as a substance that gives you great benefit when you choose wisely, listen to your Appetite, pay attention to your bodily cues, and see that your real needs are met.

Eating is a personal, individual matter. How, when, and what you feed yourself is entirely up to you. When you can choose foods based upon your tastes and desires and weigh the long-term consequences of your choices, you will be free. The food industry will no longer be able to manipulate you and your eating behavior. This is only one piece of the puzzle, but a very important one. Once you recognize the social piece, you will be in charge of you and no longer a victim. And, trust me, that will feel really good!

Most of us have not yet learned to channel the power of our Appetite. We have not yet figured out how to train it to help us instead of causing us the frustration, shame, and guilt that lead to larger clothing sizes, increased fear, and even more frustration, shame, and guilt. Meanwhile, money is spent on valid research that clearly tells us what we need to do to have healthy bodies and minds. The problem is one researcher's results often conflict with another study's findings.

Especially now with the alarming increase in incidences of obesity, type 2 diabetes, heart problems, joint pain, and many other health issues such as high blood pressure, anxiety, depression, and eating disorders in adults and children, the search continues for ways to stop and reverse the epidemic of obesity in America—home of the free, the brave, and the fattest people on the planet. This is, indeed, the land of plenty. We have plenty of food and plenty of problems resulting from our overconsumption of it. At this point, it has become a major epidemic in our culture (and many other cultures as well). There is, however, no single answer. It is about more than simply calories in and calories out. Achieving peace, balance, and ideal weight requires us to address our entire being—our physical, emotional, social, and spiritual selves as well as the environments in which we dwell.

This is a major problem all over the globe. It is, indeed, a pandemic of frightening proportions. Of course we can't "fix" the problem for everyone else in the world. It is enough to attend to ourselves. By doing so, we become role models for those around us, and this has a ripple effect, eventually reaching others who are attempting to heal from these discouraging, frustrating eating issues.

Many of us have become more confused as we have been fed more information about how to take care of ourselves, and I find that most people have no idea what "normal eating" actually is. Below is a definition to help you. It is a compilation of ideas I have pieced together from a number of sources over time that accurately describes normal eating.

NORMAL EATING

Normal eating is responding to physical cues that your body needs nourishment. It means eating until you are satisfied. Normal eating means eating foods you love and letting yourself have enough. It does not mean depriving or starving yourself because you think you *should*. Normal eating means exercising some restraint and choosing foods that are good for your body but not limiting your diet so much that you miss out on special foods you might enjoy occasionally. Normal eating means granting yourself permission to eat at any time just because you feel like it, perhaps because you feel happy or sad or because you are celebrating or mourning. It means eating sometimes for absolutely no reason other than because you want to.

On some days, normal eating means eating three meals. On other days, it could mean having more or less than that. Normal eating does, at times, mean overeating and, at other times, undereating. It means being flexible, and it means trusting yourself and your body. Normal eating means letting your body adjust to the constant fluctuations in your moods, food choices, and eating patterns. It means paying attention to your eating, but it does not mean being rigid. It does not mean worrying about your food and body excessively. Thoughts about when and what to eat are necessary in order to feed yourself well, but they should not take priority. And sometimes normal eating can mean taking care of yourself emotionally with an appropriate amount of food.

EMOTIONAL AND STRESS EATING

Emotional overeating, or stress eating, is eating primarily to mask difficult feelings. When we experience any unpleasant emotion, we may be tempted to reach for our sugar, simple carbohydrates, salt and fat fix. (By simple carbohydrates, I mean white flour and refined products, not fruits, whole grains, or vegetables.) We may also eat at any time for any reason, whether we are feeling anything in particular or not. We may be soothing our boredom or mindlessly snacking through the day. For many of us, feeding ourselves becomes disconnected from physical hunger, and at times, we may not know any other way to take care of ourselves.

When we perceive any threat to our well-being, our bodies enter in to fight or flight mode. We become tense and may not even realize it at the time. We may hold tension in our neck or shoulders or feel particularly tired and irritable. We all manifest our stress differently at different times. Some of us tend to hold it inside; others explode in angry rages. Our responses may differ, but when we are stressed, our bodies produce excess cortisol, which is a hormone that increases Appetite. This is important to know because sometimes if you realize you are extra hungry and are feeling stressed, you will know that it is in large part due to the cortisol flooding into your system, and you may choose to do something to manage your stress other than eating to soothe yourself. Change the focus of your attention. Write in your journal, put some spirited music on the stereo, watch a funny movie, go for a walk, talk with a friend, or take a warm bath, for example.

MAKE FRIENDS WITH YOURSELF

In reality, we do know what to do in every situation. The answers lie deep within us, but the barrage of messages we receive confuses us, and we doubt our own wisdom. Those marketing sugary, fatty foods or diet products tell us one thing, while those conducting solid research on exercise, nutrition, and health tell us something quite different. If we are honest with ourselves and listen to our intuition as we sift through the piles of conflicting facts, we discover the truth. We can find our own answers and empower ourselves to act in our own best interests. This is not easy to do at first, but it is possible and necessary. It is, however, impossible to act in our own best interests at every single moment. We are all human beings—all works in progress. We can strive for perfection, but we will inevitably wind up feeling like failures if we hold perfection as a goal we should or must attain. How many times have I said that already? It does bear repeating.

Please entertain this thought: You are perfect just as you are, right this minute as you are reading this page; however, you will never be able to behave perfectly in every instance. I cannot emphasize this enough! This is a truth, and it is a liberating one. If you hold this truth in your heart, it will help you on your journey to vibrant health of your body, mind, and spirit. It will enable you to work with your Appetite as a trusted partner, helping you along your journey to a healthy body and mind and a lifetime of well-being and joy, which truly is what you deserve. No one else knows what you really need. Only you do!. You can look outside of yourself for guidance, but you will be missing the point. The truth lies deep within you, and only you can determine what's best for you. Educate yourself and then use the suggestions and ideas that make sense to you. Your brilliant guidance system will never steer you wrong. If it doesn't feel true or right, it is not true or right for you.

To educate you, I will attend to many of your questions. What should I eat? What should I not eat? Why do I eat when I know I am not really hungry? How can I ever stop overeating? How can I retrieve my health and revive my spirit? How can I live my days with zest and radiant health? These are just a few of the questions I address. To do so, I reveal parts of my life experience and the stories of some of the thousands of clients I have served for more than twenty-five years as a therapist and teacher. I share the secrets of moving beyond taming to training your Appetite to work on your behalf.

I offer much of my own experience in the pages that follow for a reason. I expose myself to assure you that you are not alone in your struggles. I have spent nearly a lifetime locked inside my own self-imposed food prison. I, perhaps like you, have, at times, been both the jailer and the jailed.

During my lifetime, I have weighed slightly more than half my present weight, as I was painfully anorexic for a time. I have also weighed nearly twice my current weight and spent seven years somewhere between those extreme weights being the "best bulimic" I could be. I fed myself by alternating binge-eating episodes with periods of deprivation and often eliminated my calories through vomiting, excessive exercising, and abusing laxatives and diuretics. Although, to the outside world, I appeared successful as a popular straight-A student and later as a loving wife and mother, I was privately living in my own version of hell. No one knew the ways I was abusing myself, and I thought no one could understand or would care. How dreadful it felt to appear together and sane on the outside, while feeling crazy and disconnected on the inside. I spent many painful years feeling isolated, frightened, and fraudulent.

No matter what you weigh or how you feel or look, if thoughts of food and your body concern you more days than not, you are living in your own personal hell of helplessness and pain. After more than sixty years on this planet, I have finally broken free of my private trap of shame, guilt, and obsession. You can, too! (Please note this does not mean I eat perfectly every day. I am, as you are, always a work in progress. My Appetite is quite well-trained at this point, but I must be vigilant and continue refining and practicing the skills I have learned, for my needs, as yours, change daily as I experience life, grow, and learn more.) My experiences, thoughts, and feelings, combined with those of my clients, will help you. You may recognize some of your own thoughts and feelings as you read the stories and examples I offer you. You will feel better!

As you read, you will progress from being outer-directed to following your inner, intuitive guidance to decide which choices to make, moment by moment. You will become actively involved in paving your own path to radiant health rather than passively following the ineffective mandates of society and the diet industry, as you have in the past.

You will likely have glimmers of insight into your particular situation as you move through the stories tucked within these pages. These insights will generate ideas from deep within you—ideas that will aid you on your journey to joy and zestful living. Bear with me. Read each page, each story, and each example. Trust that what you learn will percolate around inside your mind, body, and soul. You will feel better.

LET GO OF BEING PERFECT

Many of us often feel disappointed. Life hasn't dealt us the hand we wanted. We didn't attract and marry the perfect prince (or princess) charming. We don't have perfect children, ideal jobs, or storybook homes. We didn't have the perfect parents or attend the perfect schools. Many of us haven't figured out how to arrive at, or remain at, our ideal weight. Perhaps our teeth are crooked or we have a blemish here and there. We strive to be perfect and to create the ideal world for ourselves. We rage inside because our lives never were, are not now, and never will be perfect. No life can ever live up to our expectations, hopes, and dreams. No lifetime can ever conform to our image of unrealistic perfection. We must accept this and teach it to our children. As mentioned earlier, it is vital to look forward and let go of old hurts and resentment, otherwise we stay stuck in the past and never quite make the changes we yearn to make.

What you see is what you get. There it is. You have a life. It is yours. You have a body to use while you are living this lifetime. It is yours, and it is up to you, in the here and now, to do with it as you wish. Life was and is perfect as it is. You have perhaps been dealt what you perceive as a bad hand; however, each painful or difficult experience holds its own teachings. You could not be the wise, wonderful person you are right this minute without every experience you had and every lesson you learned. You have passed many of the classes you have taken in this earthly school. Please give yourself credit; the curriculum is not an easy one. You have clearly identified what you do not want, and in the process, you have become more aware of what you do want, even though this may not always feel clear to you in the moment.

PUT YOUR NEEDS FIRST

Why is something so basic and natural so difficult? It seems so simple to say we must make ourselves number one on our list of people to care for. It only makes sense that we do. The better we attend to ourselves, the better we feel. The better we feel, the more pleasant we are to be around, and the more connected we are to others. We thrive and our self-esteem improves when we are in healthy relationships. We have more energy and more fun, and it just gets better and better. All those around us benefit from our good feelings as well. We radiate love and happiness, and paradoxically, we become better equipped not only to handle the demands of our lives, but also to take care of others that we may choose to care for.

This is how it is. The more we pay attention to ourselves and keep ourselves feeling positive, the more energy we have to attend to others. Attention is not a limited commodity. Many of us think that if we are cherishing and honoring ourselves, we are somehow diminishing others. This makes no sense, but most of us may never have stopped to think of it in this way. The exact opposite is true. Think of the Law of Attraction, which states, "That which is like unto itself is drawn" (or "like attracts like"). Therefore, the more positive thoughts you have, the more positive you feel, and the more positive experiences and feelings you attract to yourself. When you are in this place of positive energy, you have an abundance of energy to share.

The opposite is equally true. If you deprive yourself through dieting and neglecting your own needs, you will not be very happy.

When you are feeing unhappy, you are attracting more negative experiences and feelings of unhappiness to you, and your negative feelings expand. You feel discouraged, tired, and have little or no energy. You are not able to take care of yourself very well and are certainly not in the mood to take care of anyone else. This usually results in feelings of guilt and shame, lowered self-esteem, and increased negativity.

So why is it so hard to make yourself number one? I often ask women who come into my office where they are on their list of priorities and often discover that they are either very close to the bottom or not on their list at all. They profess that their waking hours are consumed with important tasks they must complete for their families and friends and to meet the demands of their jobs. Some of these women have children to care for. Some do not. Some have jobs that require much time and attention. Some do not. But what all have in common is a distinct inability to attend to their own important needs.

Ignoring their own needs explains why women so often grab sugar, simple carbohydrates, salt and fat to dull their feelings. If you are living your life in service of everyone else and neglecting yourself, you are telling yourself that you do not deserve to be treated as well as others. You are giving yourself a clear message that you are not important, and somewhere deep inside, you know that you are! It is inevitable that you will feel resentful and negative, and as mentioned above, you will attract more negative feelings and find yourself more eager than ever to wrap your hand around a big chocolate bar. You know you can count on the sweet relief it will deliver—at least for a few minutes. It will distract you from your feelings, but what will you do after that pleasant numbing wears off?

STEP III – Take 100% Responsibility

You are not a victim. These are your options. You can continue to focus outwardly on everyone else and devote all your precious time to others. You realize, however, that by doing so, you are setting yourself up for more pain and resentment. You might even consider buying stock in your favorite candy company and arranging for automatic home delivery of the sweet of your choice because you will definitely eat quite a bit. You also will want to set money aside to buy the larger sizes of clothing you will need.

Alternatively, you can make some important changes and rearrange your priorities. I don't simply want you to move your name up on your list of priorities. I want you to put it at the very top—above everybody else's! Is this impossible? No! I want you to make a firm commitment to yourself to spend at least half an hour on yourself every single day. That is not much time at all. Women are adamant that there is no free time in their busy lives to do so. I can empathize with these women, having single-parented three children while going to school and working full time. I know from experience that this is not an easy request.

I tell my clients that they will never find the time. If they wait for extra time to appear in their schedules or they plan to use leftover time, they will never have any time for themselves. Instead, they must take their time off the top. Making time for yourself has to be top priority. If you do not make it so, then it will never happen. I strongly suggest that you think of what time of day you have your best energy and schedule your half hour then. Plan everything else around your time. Set strong, impenetrable boundaries, and stick to your resolve on this one. If you have set one to one thirty in the afternoon as your time, for example, you must show up and not allow anything to interfere.

When I first decided to give myself some time, I recognized that my very best energy was first thing in the morning. I was in the habit of getting up at six, and I needed to get up then to make my children breakfast, pack their lunches and see them out the door and off to school. It did occur to me that I could get up at five thirty, but that seemed horribly early. I reasoned that I needed that extra half hour in bed because my life was so exhausting and demanding. I needed all the rest I could get.

Yet, I thought it was worth a try, so one night, before climbing into bed, I set my alarm for five thirty. The first morning, I think I hit my snooze button ten times and never set a foot on the floor until after six. Then I was even more tired and in a rush to get everything done. The next morning, however, I did get out of my warm, cozy bed at five thirty, and what a surprise I had in store! My home was quiet and peaceful, and I discovered the magic of sitting quietly and undisturbed while I did exactly as I pleased. I loved the time for myself so much that it didn't take me long to start getting up at five.

Truthfully, even though it has been many years since I've had children at home, I now get up at four every morning, and I love it! It is the very best time of day. It is all mine to enjoy as I please. I give myself this gift of time without hesitation, because I do love myself (almost all the time) and know that I both need and deserve it. Often, women tell me that taking precious time just for themselves seems selfish. Not only is it not selfish it is essential!

ARE YOU BEING SELFISH OR SELF-LOVING?

There is a difference between being selfish and self-loving. Women often confuse the two. Being self-loving is attending to your own needs, making yourself as important—not less or more important—as everyone else. From this place of equality springs the desire for equal treatment. This means you care for yourself and give to yourself, not just focus your time and attention on others. You treat yourself well and lavish yourself with nurturing attention. You will then have more desire and more energy for completing tasks and lovingly caring for others.

Being selfish means disregarding everyone else's needs and taking whatever you want with no consideration of them and their rights. Being selfish does not feel good, but being self-loving does. Feeling good is the most important thing for you to strive for. Recall that feeling good leads to more good feelings, more positive experiences, and more energy. This results in you giving more to yourself and, next, to others.

When you make yourself number one, you create a win-win situation for everybody. When you act selfishly, with no regard for others, you create the opposite—a lose-lose situation. In the latter case, you don't feel happy. You radiate negative energy, feel depleted and exhausted, and no one feels good—not you or anyone else.

When you keep your needs in the forefront of your mind, you do everyone a great service. You are modeling self-loving behavior. You are feeling better, and as a result, you may be surprised to find that everyone around you will be feeling more positive as well. It is infectious. The happier you are, the more you radiate joy, and the more those around you will become joyful.

If you have negative relationships in your life, they may change when you consistently stay in a positive-feeling state, also known as a positive vibration. If you have people in your life who insist on focusing primarily on the negative, let them know that you will not join them in their negativity. You can tell them that this does not feel good and does not serve you well. They may or may not understand, and there is a chance you could lose those relationships. Since negative relationships drain your energy and pull you into negative vibration, this is a good thing. If someone leaves you because they can't support you doing what is good for you, then ask yourself what you were doing in that relationship in the first place.

We all need supportive, growth-promoting connections in our lives. We do not live happily in isolation. We are social beings, and our relationships are of utmost importance. If you are experiencing conflict in a relationship, it is wise for you to first look at your own behaviors before pointing a finger at the other person. Give yourself a time-out so you have the necessary space and time you need to think about how your feelings and actions are affecting the relationship. This is difficult, as we'd much prefer it to be entirely the other person's fault, but it never is. We always have our part. It then takes courage to go to the other person, take responsibility for our behavior, and admit our part of the problem.

If, after honestly examining your own motives and resulting actions, you feel you are, indeed, coming from an honest, open-hearted place and the conflict cannot be resolved or it intensifies, you may need to visit a counselor together, and ultimately, you may need to move on. You need to do whatever is necessary to nurture yourself and meet your own needs.

This is important because women are often expected to be the caretakers of everyone around them, which leaves little time to take care of themselves. Because women's energy can easily become drained in service to others, they seldom, if ever, apportion time to nurture themselves. This leaves precious little time remaining to stop and pay attention to what their inner guidance system, their intuition, is trying to communicate.

I want to emphasize the importance of setting and maintaining clear, impenetrable boundaries. Step-by-step directions are provided later on to help you take the very best care of yourself. Basic skills for managing stress are scattered throughout the book, and I encourage you to adopt the strategies that sound most helpful to you. In doing so, you make yourself number one, and paradoxically you have greater energy reserves for others as well.

MAKE FRIENDS WITH YOUR APPETITE

What does it mean to befriend your Appetite, and why is it important? The basic premise is as follows:

- Your Appetite transmits constant streams of messages to you, which frequently are not about actual hunger.

- If you simply pay attention to the hunger messages and attempt to satiate yourself with food, you have missed important communications from your internal guidance system. You are likely to remain hungry and not feel satisfied.

- When you befriend your Appetite and pay close attention to the valuable communications it brings, you begin to value your Appetite as a true friend who brings you important messages instead of regarding it as a foe.

- Because your desires extend far beyond controlling both your food intake and your weight, your Appetite begins to work beside you to encourage you along the path to radiant health, joy, balance, and the creation of the life you truly desire.

- To craft your ideal life, you must be clear about what your desires actually are and learn to be positive as much as possible. Then, as the Law of Attraction assures, you will attract positive experiences and feelings. (I will further explain the Law of Attraction and how to use it in Step IV.)

- Your Appetite will become friendly, loyal, and playful and will stand beside you. It will alert you vigilantly when you are on the right track, moving toward achieving your life goals, or when you are not. It will constantly and faithfully deliver messages from your internal guidance system about what choices are in your best interest in all aspects of your life.

Think of your Appetite as a wild horse for a minute. If you yank a mustang off the range, it will do all in its power to get away. It will panic and behave with terrible fury. It will snort and buck erratically as it tries with all its might to escape. If you ever want this horse to be useful to you and become your friend, you will have to tame it before you can train it. This is a mighty task!

Thoughts of an actual wild horse conjure up images of speed and power with dust flying and hooves flailing as the animal rears and bucks in protest against being caught and tamed. Our Appetite can feel just as out of control and powerful if we don't understand it. Many of us have spent our lives trying to tame our wild urges to overeat, and many of us have failed to bring our Appetites under control and have gained weight, or at least failed to lose weight, as a result.

Taming a horse takes patience. We must first make friends with the frightened animal and begin to develop trust. If we beat it or treat it unkindly, our chances of ever gaining its trust disappear, or at least diminish significantly. The process is not about domination over the animal, but instead about establishing a working, cooperative relationship with it. Gradually, as we treat the animal with gentle, loving care, we may be able to cautiously slip a halter over its head and guide it slowly with a lead rope. This process, this taming, does not happen overnight, nor does the process of taming our wild urges to overeat. This resistant, stubborn, wild, powerful part of each of us is what I refer to as our saboteur, Chew, or insatiable, out-of-control Appetite.

In my previous book, *The Taming of the Chew*, I outlined valuable steps toward identifying and making friends with and taming your Chew. (You will find a synopsis of that work at the end of this section. And, remember, your Chew also means your Appetite.) Much like training a wild horse, you must not beat yourself up or be mean to yourself. You must be patient and gentle with yourself if you are to first tame and then train your Appetite. This is your first step: Adopt an attitude of kindness toward yourself. Only then will you be able to move ahead.

There are basic skills necessary for successfully taming your Appetite and stopping compulsive overeating behavior. General reasons for overeating develop from physical, emotional, social, and spiritual issues, and many ways to change your eating habits and heal yourself—again, on physical, emotional, social, and spiritual levels—are outlined in this book. Once you read these suggestions, you will be ready to go further—to progress from merely taming your Appetite to actually training it to work in your best interests.

Just as a well-trained horse is a pleasure to own and ride, a well-trained Appetite can become your friend and be pleasurable as well. This is difficult to imagine at first. We think of our saboteur, Appetite or Chew, as evil; most people wish they could eliminate it entirely, as it represents those unruly urges to gobble up everything in sight. Of course, you cannot make your Appetite disappear, but as you learn to train it, it will begin sending you constant messages about how you are doing and how to take the best care of yourself.

It will become your partner and work in your best interests *with* you instead of *against* you.

There are distinct steps you must take to properly train a horse. Once you have tamed this magnificent animal and are able to guide it along with a lead rope, you might put a saddle on it and walk it around as it gets used to the strange feeling of a foreign object on its back. When you think your horse is ready to go further, you can introduce it to a bridle and bit. You wouldn't take this horse with which you have been working to develop a trusting relationship and jam a bit into its mouth, nor would you beat it into submission. This would undo all of your patient efforts. Likewise, you must learn not to be harsh with yourself or expect to adopt new behaviors overnight.

It takes time to adjust and train yourself successfully, just as training a horse takes time. It may take a month or more just to become friends with it. Patience is the key. When the day comes that you swing your leg up and sit in the saddle, you feel proud of both yourself and your animal. At first, someone else may lead your horse with you in the saddle, and eventually, you can hold the reins and ride on your own. As you feel the thrill of that moment, you know your patience and hard work have paid off.

At that time, you can begin working with your animal to teach it how to respond to your commands. Horses can run, jump, or trot by themselves, but you must train them when and how you want them to do these things. Also, horses don't turn right or left by sensing the direction in which you would like to move. You must teach them, and with great patience, you must help them master each small step before moving on to the next.

When you are finally able to mount your horse and ride with confidence, you must still regularly attend to the needs of your animal. If you fail to keep up your training, your horse will forget. You must be vigilant with habitual riding and training sessions to keep your horse performing as you wish, just as you will need to heed the messages of your Appetite and be watchful of yourself.

And so it is with each of us. We must master one step at a time and exercise great patience and gentle care as we move step by step into a better, healthier life experience. Once we have befriended and trained our Appetite, we can check in with ourselves regularly to determine how we are doing. Then we will not just be moving toward greater health, perfect weight, and a delicious life of balance and joy, but we will be happily prancing along! By reading this book, you are finding out how.

BEGINNING WITH *THE TAMING OF THE CHEW*

The following is a brief recap of *The Taming of the Chew*. I present this because it provides a base of knowledge to help you use the coming suggestions more easily and effectively. As you read the synopsis below, proceed slowly and think carefully about how these statements match your experiences. You will learn much about yourself, your lifestyle, and your Appetite as you pause and reflect on each topic. If you have already read *The Taming of the Chew*, please peruse this section as a valuable review.

Reasons for Overeating

Physical
Many of us fail to feed ourselves well. We receive so much conflicting information about how to nourish our bodies that it is often difficult to sift through it all and design a healthy eating plan for ourselves.

It is difficult for most of us to fit exercise of any kind into our already overburdened schedules. It is imperative, however, that we make time to move our bodies. Exercise is important for strengthening muscles and burning calories, but we also reap enormous benefits emotionally. When we exercise, our bodies release natural chemicals called endorphins that serve as powerful, effective antianxiety agents and/or antidepressant medications. Exercising regularly helps with overall health, not just with weight management. You will find yourself calmer and more peaceful, and you will experience energy that is magnificent and not frenetic.

People are sometimes ignorant about the importance of staying hydrated, getting ample amounts of good-quality sleep, and taking advantage of the benefits of sunshine. All of these are necessary to achieve health and maintain an optimal body weight. When we do not get a sufficient amount of sleep, our body secretes excess ghrelin and reduces the amount of leptin it usually provides. These two hormones are key players in regulating Appetite. Excess ghrelin, the hunger hormone, causes increased Appetite. When the body reduces the production of leptin, the satiation hormone, we don't feel satisfied. We also become more vulnerable to stress, and we release excess cortisol, another hormone that increases hunger.

Therefore, when we don't get adequate sleep, we are likely overly hungry and fail to feel satisfied. Did you ever realize that lack of good-quality sleep could affect your Appetite in this way? Please get a good amount of sound sleep. Go to bed at a regular time, preferably before ten. Darken your room, fill your mind with positive thoughts, and relax. If sleep eludes you and your mind is rehashing the worries and problems of the day, try two sprays of Rescue Sleep on your tongue or a few drops of this tincture in a beverage. (There is more information about using Bach® Flower Remedies in Step IV.)

If sleeping is consistently difficult for you after following these suggestions, please discuss this problem with your doctor. He or she may want to arrange an appointment for you at a sleep center, where your sleep patterns can be evaluated. If you are not getting quality sleep at night, experts there can make suggestions to help you start getting the rest you so badly need.

Emotional

It is often difficult for women to access, identify, and express true feelings, especially anger, because we were never encouraged to express ourselves fully or were never appreciated for doing so if we tried.

It is often difficult to communicate with others. Women frequently report feeling invalidated, exploited, and devalued when they have attempted to make their thoughts and feelings known. They fear full expression of themselves because they fear they will be ignored or alienate others, incurring their wrath and anger, which, for many of us, is terrifying to experience.

Research has shown that women's self-esteem depends on our ability to make and maintain growth-fostering, mutually empathic, reciprocal connections in all our relationships. This makes it extremely difficult for us to risk any word or behavior that might—real or imagined—alienate anyone with whom we are choosing to have a relationship.

Social

In this culture, women are bombarded with messages from endless sources about how to look, what to feel, and exactly how to behave. To be fully accepted in this culture, we must be young, thin, cheerful, and compliant, but also independent, strong, and able to multitask flawlessly. This, of course, sets us up with unrealistic expectations of ourselves. We are bound to fail if we continue to strive for the approval and recognition from others that we imagine will enrich our lives and enhance our connections. Like it or not, happiness is an inside job.

Spiritual

Many of us have been carefully taught to look outside of ourselves to determine our spiritual path. We may have adopted the practices of a particular theological orientation only to find ourselves dissatisfied because the beliefs and teachings we were offered didn't feel right to us. Many of us never learned how to tap into our spiritual essence and connect with our spirit. (If you are a member of a religion that feels true and comfortable for you, that is wonderful. In addition to that belief system, you might consider enriching your spirit in other ways as well.)

Due to our fast-paced culture, many women are generally busy taking care of others, while at the same time often working full or part time, and they find precious little time to devote to themselves. This can result in women experiencing a life that is not personally rewarding or fulfilling. Whether we are caring for others or not, many of us overeat to medicate the feelings of boredom and disappointment that result from neglecting ourselves.

Life feels wonderful when we can balance our need to attend to ourselves with attending to others' needs. It is when we allow others' needs to crowd ours out of the picture that a problem results. If we don't attend to our physical, emotional, social and spiritual needs, we won't have fun; we will not have the joyful, delicious lives we are intended to have. The less fun and joy we feel, the more we will be tempted to abuse ourselves with food.

Following is a recap of some of the suggestions for healing found in *The Taming of the Chew*: Think about each suggestion. How many can you implement right now? What changes do you want or need to make to move in a positive, healthy direction?

Ways to Heal

Physical:

- Exercise moderately every day. Move. Have fun.

- Drink plenty of pure water to stay hydrated at all times.

- Give yourself an adequate amount of good-quality sleep.

- Expose yourself to sunshine daily to receive a healthy dose of vitamin D.

Emotional:

- Learn good communication and assertiveness skills and practice them daily. There are many self-help books available on these topics, and classes are sometimes offered to help participants hone their skills.

- When you feel the urge to overeat, pay attention to what you are feeling in order to decide what you really need at the time. Chances are it is not actually food.

- Develop a repertoire of ways to soothe yourself that do not include food, like taking long walks, reading a good novel, etc.

Social:

- Examine your own perfectionistic self-expectations.

- Set realistic goals that are challenging, but attainable, not impossible.

- Challenge the socialization messages you have received and question the inconsistent communications you are being bombarded with.

- Learn to think for yourself.

Spiritual:

- Take a good amount of private time for yourself every day.

- Make time to have fun and be creative.

- Revisit your priorities and spend more time engaged in activities that please you.

- Play, laugh, dance, enjoy life, and don't be so serious!

As you discover many of your personal reasons for overeating and some effective ways to rein in those urges, you will be successfully taming your Appetite. But be aware that urges to overeat are still likely to surface at times despite your best, most sincere efforts. Why is it not enough to tame your Appetite? Why is it imperative to move to another deeper level and train it to help you instead of continuing to hurt you?

Once you have tamed your Appetite by learning why you behave as you do and implementing some effective strategies for change, you are well equipped to move from taming to training your Appetite to work in your best interests instead of against you.

Let's say that, at this point, you have built a fair amount of trust with your wild horse. You tamed it enough to allow you to place a bit in its mouth and put a saddle on its back, maybe you even climbed into the saddle. You have made outstanding progress. Now you are ready to move beyond the basic phases of taming and beginner training to the exciting advanced process of training your magnificent animal to behave and perform as you wish and work with you as a team.

You are now ready to train your Appetite to perform as an ally and friend instead of as an oppositional, frustrating, problematic saboteur. As you proceed through the remaining pages of this book, you will learn many ways to do this. It is essential, however, that you must be equally patient and loving with yourself, just as you must proceed slowly, patiently, and lovingly with your animal's training. You expect there will be days when you accomplish much with your horse and other days when things may not progress as smoothly. Remember, this will also be true for you as you and your Appetite learn to function together as a team working in your best interests.

Some days will be more difficult than others. Those days are equally valuable, however, as you learn ways to make the next day more successful. As you reframe your thinking to include the idea of working with your Appetite instead of against it, you no longer have to battle your bucking-bronco Appetite into submission. You will finally be able to give up the food-control struggle you have been engaged in for so long. You will be free!

STEP IV – Gather Your Tools

Y ou may notice that this step is lengthy and makes up a large portion of the second half of this book. This is because this step contains a plethora of important information and ideas you can use to change negative, self-destructive behaviors into a succession of positive, growth-promoting choices that will lead you into your delicious life.

Aren't you tired of looking around to find the answer to your eating problems? As a culture, we have learned to expect quick fixes. If we have a headache, we take a pill and the headache disappears. If we want something new, we buy it. If we are hungry, the choices are endless. We have come to expect instant gratification, so when we are shown a piece of new exercise equipment or learn of a revolutionary diet or weight-loss pill, we eagerly jump on the bandwagon.

There is nothing we want more than a magic answer, and these products promise us exactly that. Of course, they can't deliver, as real change takes time, patience and a willingness to put forth effort. We are all smart enough to know this, yet we still get hooked by the instant results we are promised on our television screens.

To truly change, we have to get to know ourselves and treat ourselves with kindness and respect. The first step is becoming friendly with our feelings.

MAKE FRIENDS WITH YOUR FEELINGS

Experiencing what you are feeling is crucial to training your Appetite, for only with the knowledge of your feelings can you make the very best, self-loving choices. When I ask, "Do you take the time to feel your feelings?" most people answer yes. They imply with their tone of voice and facial expression that my question is a foolish one. You may be agreeing with them as you read this; however, as in the case of Michelle, who thought she had to be perfect, with the busy lives we lead, precious little time is spent acknowledging and attending to our feelings.

For one thing, we seldom, if ever, experience only one feeling at a time. In fact, we often flood with assorted emotions. It can feel too difficult, even overwhelming, to discern what our true feelings are and then decipher the messages they are trying so hard to deliver to us. Even as we are trying to figure out what we're feeling, more feelings are coming along. These persistent feelings make up our internal guidance system and, as such, are constantly providing the information we require to make the very best choices for ourselves in each moment. To take full advantage of these important messages, we must pay close attention to what we are feeling and heed the instructions we are being given. We often find ourselves in situations where our feelings are running rampant, and we may not even realize it. It is helpful at those times to stop and figure out exactly what we are feeling and what our intuition is telling us.

For example, most of us have instant replays in our mind and hearts when we hear terms like 9/11, tsunami, Katrina, Iraq, earthquakes, fires, and floods. When our ears hear the words and our eyes view the pictures, our whole being reacts. Emotions instantly surface, and we are flooded with an array of feelings. We may feel frightened, unsafe, helpless, furious, overwhelmed, or sad, just to name a few possible reactions, for others as well as for ourselves. We may feel relieved that we have survived, while at the same time feel guilty that we have survived when others have not. We may become depressed and anxious and not understand why.

As human beings, we are acting and reacting all the time. Part of us may try to actively suppress or deny our uncomfortable feelings, while another part of us may be reacting to the news by grieving or feeling angry. There is no one right way to react or to feel. When we are experiencing intense emotions, some of which we understand and some we don't, the end result is distress. Hearing of and witnessing the suffering of others causes stress, and we may turn to old, unhealthy patterns in search of relief. We may seek food for comfort. Millions of us do!

This is a natural reaction, by the way, so please don't beat yourself up if you have indulged in a few extra snacks lately. There is plenty of distressing news reaching you via all forms of the media and in the personal experiences you have every day. As you know, we learned at a tender age that sugar, simple carbohydrates, salt and fat will take away our pain. These substances mask themselves as our friends. They urge us to take care of our uncomfortable feelings by stuffing our bellies with creamy pastas, pastries, and chocolate—and they work. They deliver the sweet relief they promise. These foods help us in the short term; however, we are only stuffing our feelings deep inside, where we don't have to cope with them— yet. They will surface again later and continue to do so until we deal with them head-on.

When the effects of our "anesthetics" wear off, our physical bodies scream for more, and our emotional selves, which haven't yet recognized and experienced our emotions, join the chorus and demand more "treats" to continue keeping our feelings at bay. Some of us may turn to the use of alcohol, sex, gambling, or drugs to avoid the complex emotions of everyday life. Some of us are more likely to head for the corner coffee shop to grab a muffin and a latte or to use any other combination of escape mechanisms.

Remind yourself that your feelings exist for a reason. Each feeling is telling you something. Each is bringing you valuable information about what's going on around and within you. Listen. Experience your feelings, and let yourself feel every high and low that life brings your way. No one ever said that life meant experiencing only pleasant emotions. In fact, we need the difficult ones to appreciate the joyous ones.

If you do choose—and it is a choice, though it may not feel like one at the time—to soothe yourself with food, please don't beat yourself up when you are done. That *never* helps! None of us can walk our paths perfectly at all times. We are all human, and we all make less-than-self-loving choices at times. Move beyond the urge to punish yourself. Recall that there are no mistakes, only lessons. Be as gentle as possible with yourself first, and then do what you realistically can to help others who have experienced trauma. Listen to them. Pray for them and with them. Share hugs, warm smiles, resources, and words of encouragement.

And remind yourself that life flies by. It is a blink of time. Amidst the stress and turmoil, tap into the peace and quiet strength within yourself. Bypass unhealthy choices as often as you can, and don't beat yourself if occasionally you can't. Most importantly, appreciate each moment of this exciting, emotional, and sometimes turbulent journey!

It is crucial to do so as you strive to find joy and balance. If you feel cold, you put on a coat. If you are thirsty, you get something to drink. Finding happiness is your life's purpose and your most important task. You need to experience the discomfort of too hot or too cold in order to know what a comfortable temperature level feels like. You require the experience of hunger or thirst to recognize satiation. You are wired to listen and respond to the messages your body sends you.

Chances are you have heard this before, but have you ever really stopped to think about it? That is what I am asking you to do now— just think about it. Think of how wondrous our bodies and emotions are as they constantly provide the necessary, valuable guidance we need to make choices in our own best interests. If we just stop, pay attention, and heed the messages our emotions are delivering rather than stuffing them away with food, we will be crafting our delicious lives of vibrant health and happiness.

Every cell in our entire body contains an intelligence of its own. That is why our digestion takes place without us seeming to do anything, how our lungs know how to breathe, and why our hair grows longer. Our cells just know what to do, and each cell has its own specific job. These miraculous little cells are always busy regulating what flows in and out of them. For example, if a cell contains too much potassium, it will pump some out and bring more in later if it needs to. This process of regulation that each cell performs so beautifully and naturally helps the cell to achieve and maintain necessary balance, or homeostasis. As larger organisms, we must do the same, always adapting to changes in our environments as well as within ourselves.

We are busy people, and with each new time-saving gadget that is invented, we get busier. Our thoughts and feelings then become more congested and harder to decipher. It is not only prudent, but also essential to slow down and untangle the many thoughts and feelings we are having if we are to make sense of them and follow the wise guidance they are trying so hard to provide to us. If we do not *make* the time—not *find* the time because we will never just *find* the time—to access and name our feelings, we are likely to find ourselves thoughtlessly engaging in overeating behavior to quiet the noise and confusion we are experiencing inside.

It may feel overwhelming to us to slow down and focus within ourselves to figure out what our internal experience is at the moment. We are not accustomed to changing our focus from the many things that are going on outside of ourselves to that which we are experiencing within ourselves. We can learn to do this. As each cell of our body constantly accommodates its ever-changing needs in seeking homeostasis, we must make necessary adjustments to meet our own needs and maintain emotional balance.

Stop and consider what you are feeling at this moment. If you are not accustomed to this sort of self-reflection and find this task difficult, that is fine. You will be able to do this in time. Quietly practice tuning in to yourself and following your intuition, noticing your feelings as often as you can throughout the day. You will become more and more in touch with what your real needs are from one moment to the next, and thoughts of food will diminish. They will recede into the background as your real needs are called to the foreground. Then you can choose the very best actions to take to give yourself what you are truly craving.

It is human nature to soothe ourselves when we feel bad; likewise, it is human nature to treat ourselves when we are happy. We have constant opportunities to do so, and we are likely to choose unhealthy foods under both of these circumstances. Food is the focal point of nearly every occasion, and the sweet, addictive, mind-numbing foods that encourage overindulgence are the most popular. There are reasons why. We get busier and busier every day; however, we are not Energizer Bunnies. We are humans who spend much time *doing* and not much time *being*. When we fill our bodies with nutritionally barren junk food, we numb ourselves, zone out, and feel little. The pressures of the day recede temporarily into the background, and we smile and nap and automatically reach for more anesthetic foods to keep the edge off our feelings.

These unhealthy foods are serving a purpose for us—a purpose many of us have come to rely on. They are helping us calm down and stop the rush of the chaotic thoughts and feelings that we were likely in the middle of when we grabbed the first bite. But, at the same time, aren't we keeping our feelings muted, our thinking fuzzy, and ourselves out of touch with the wonder and joy of being alive?

What if we went without our customary sugar, simple carbo-hydrates, salt and fat fix? What if we actually took the time to stop and think and take full responsibility for our feelings, choices, and actions? Concerns about our bodies and what we are eating, or about to eat, may distract us from thinking about other, perhaps more important, things. What would happen in your life if you resigned as the busiest person in your family, workplace, neighbor-hood, or school? Chances are the world would still spin on its axis, and life on Earth would continue.

Ask yourself if your services are really as important as you think. Do you really need to be this busy? You are, indeed, a very impor-tant person, but what purpose is it serving for you to race mindlessly through your life at breakneck speed taking care of everyone and everything else and trying to do it all perfectly? Why keep charging toward that unattainable goal of perfection? It is an automatic setup for failure. Why not slow down, relax, and focus for a while on what *you* truly want? Why not do this several times a day? It will become a habit that will serve you well.

How wonderful that you are taking the time to read this book and to stop and think about yourself right now. Forget what you have done in the past. You can transform yourself and your life in an instant if you choose to. This may seem impossible, even though desirable, but you really can. You will need to slow down, however, and then begin to implement the following three suggestions:

- <u>Stop, Look, and Listen</u>: It is vital to pay attention to your-self and your surroundings in order to get a clear under-standing of what you want.

- <u>Consider Your Choices</u>: Be aware that you have choices and the power to choose exactly what you want to say or do. You are not a victim!

- <u>Express Yourself</u>: You will need to communicate your thoughts and feelings in order to connect with others and be heard and understood.

Following these three suggestions is necessary for your well-being. Let me explain.

STOP, LOOK, AND LISTEN

Pause long enough to notice your surroundings. Notice the colors, the scents, the sounds, and all the details. Allow yourself to tune in to the full experience of just being wherever you are at the moment. Then quiet your mind by taking some slow, deep breaths and begin to notice what feelings are percolating around inside you. You are likely experiencing a number of things. Try to identify some of the most powerful feelings. (It may help to write them down.) Then as you acknowledge these feelings to yourself, you can fully tune in to the experience you are having at the moment.

For example, you might say, "I notice I feel tired and over-whelmed. I didn't sleep well last night, and I have been worrying a lot about my job (or relationship or money or health or something else). I feel tension in my neck and shoulders, and I am cranky and short-tempered this morning." As you notice these things, you position yourself to decide what you truly need to do to take the best care of yourself in that moment. In the past, you have most likely used food to dull these important feeling messages, and you have missed the chance to identify your real needs. You may find you are tempted to grab a few crackers or some chocolate when you do this exercise. Your reaction is natural if eating has become the primary way you have been meeting your emotional needs. But perhaps you can defer that automatic response of food abuse and instead think of what else might better meet your needs.

Noticing your feelings and taking time to pay attention to them is the most important part of making the decisions that will help you as you continually strive for balance and joy in your life. Using the valuable information your feelings provide for you helps you create the experience you truly desire. This is part of the training process. It is at those times that your Appetite is working with you and helping you identify what you really want and need for your own peace, health, and well-being.

CONSIDER YOUR CHOICES

Remind yourself that although your energy is low and life feels particularly difficult in this moment, you do have options. Have a conversation with yourself. For example, you might say, "Yes, I notice I am tired and discouraged and fearful right now. What would be the very best, most effective, and gentle way to take care of my true needs at this particular time? Perhaps I can call my friend and talk a while or go for a walk with my dog or take a nap. Maybe I just need a little quiet time to regroup, meditate, write in my journal, pray, or cry. What is it I am really craving if I bypass my usual, mind-numbing sugar, carbohydrates, salt and fat fix? Do I need stimulation or relaxation, isolation or socialization? Do I need protein or more water or a little sunshine? Do I need to attend to some unfinished business? Do I need to tell someone how I feel?" There are many possibilities and each time you go through this process you are taking giant steps toward helping your Appetite to serve you and to work with you to accomplish your life goals.

Practice stopping and thinking about what would truly serve you best in that moment. When you are attentive to yourself in this way, you feel better, and food becomes less important. It only takes a moment, but it is an essential moment. As Dr. Kessler points out, to do this requires that you quiet down and focus within to tap into your intuition and discover what pleases you. Otherwise, you will remain focused outwardly, and you will find yourself reacting to stimuli around you instead of acting on your own behalf.

Once you develop the habit of this intuitive check-in with your inner self, you find the peace and balance you are striving for, and your body adjusts to the weight that is perfect for you. Your Appetite becomes a source of joy for you instead of frustration. And one of the greatest benefits is that you feel proud of yourself. You smile more, and people notice how radiant you have become!

EXPRESS YOURSELF

Many of us never learned how to communicate authentically within ourselves or with others. As we practice the skill of attending to our inner being and listening to our feeling messages, we are likely to discover that we want and need to communicate more honestly, clearly, and fully with those around us. This is not easy for many of us. Most of us were taught to be quiet from an early age. (Children should be seen and not heard!) If we did dare to speak up, we may have been reprimanded, ridiculed, or discounted.

Our precious thoughts may have been negated and our feelings invalidated. Soon we learned to withhold our true thoughts and bury our feelings deep inside—so deep that we may have lost touch with them ourselves. These consequences of our self-expression were painful, and it didn't take us long to realize and appreciate the soothing relief we could find with a few cookies or a big dish of ice cream.

Now, when it is important for us to speak up as adults, we may feel afraid. This is understandable given the ways our communication may have been received in the past. What is your worst fear if you speak up in the particular situation that concerns you? Is this fear realistic? What's the worst thing that could really happen? Sometimes knowing what your greatest fear is can dispel the power you have given away in anticipation of a confrontation or rejection.

It is far easier to swallow a brownie than to tell your neighbor you don't want to care for her child again. But if you don't speak up, and she doesn't happen to be a mind reader, nothing will change, and you will likely go on eating an endless supply of sweets, gaining weight, and harboring greater resentment toward her for taking advantage of you and toward yourself for allowing her to. Then you will need more anesthetic sugar, carbohydrates, salt and fat fixes to keep that anger and resentment at bay.

It is necessary that you learn to assert yourself and communicate what your wants and needs truly are. You deserve to ask for what you want and express yourself. Your feelings are no more or less important than anyone else's. You can always ask for what you need and express all that you wish to express. This precious earthly life is yours, and you are responsible for creating the experience you want. Others around you are responsible for creating their own life experiences. You can't live your life to serve their needs to the exclusion of your own and still feel happy, nor can you expect others to read your mind, discover what your needs are, and live their lives in service to you. Each of us must make our own choices and create the most positive, joyful life possible.

Here is a simple communication formula that many find helpful to express their thoughts and feelings:

(feeling)   (behavior)
I feel _____ when you _____.

For example, "I feel angry when you leave your clothes all over the floor." To use this formula effectively, you will first need to learn how to recognize and name your feelings. Always begin your statement with the words "I feel." If you start by saying "you," the other person is likely to feel threatened and tune you out on the spot. Starting with "I feel" instead opens the door to productive communication and invites the other person to listen. Be clear that you name a true feeling that you are experiencing. Statements like, "I feel like you're a jerk," are not likely to be helpful!

Once you are clear about how you feel, you can then name a specific behavior that you would like to address with the other person. In a perfect world, he or she might respond to your communication by saying something such as, "Oh, I am sorry. I will now pick up my clothes since I now know you don't like me to leave them on the floor." Chances of that happening, however, are slim. Usually, you will have to tell them more than once. If they still do not respond to your request after two or three talks, it is time to add a consequence to the communication formula:

$$(feeling) \qquad (behavior)$$
I feel _____ when you _____, and if you

$$(consequence)$$
continue, I will _____.

For example, "I feel angry when you leave your clothes all over the floor, and if you continue, I will throw them out the bathroom window." Now, your consequence must be appropriate to the crime and something you can actually do. Then you *must* follow through. If you communicate clearly using this technique, people will begin to take you seriously, and you will no longer feel helpless and invisible. Try it and see!

There are a few important things, however, to think about before you use the formula. First, it may not be healthy for you to associate your feelings with another's behavior all the time. Personal growth involves learning to separate who we are and how we feel about ourselves from another's behavior. Setting a boundary is different. We need to be clear about what we want and communicate that. The communication formula may be most useful for you if you have trouble letting others know how you feel, but be prepared that it is not a magic answer, and you may make yourself more vulnerable. The person you are sharing your feelings with may not appreciate or respect them.

What do you do if the other person doesn't cooperate with you? What if they don't care about your feelings? Your "I" statement could generate the opposite effect from what you are trying to achieve. Be judicious about when you use the formula. If you think your feelings will be used against you, then consider other ways to let the person know what you want, leaving your feelings out of it. Also, I advise against using this formula very often with children. Whether you say you are angry at them about something or pleased with them when they perform well, you are telling them that they are responsible for your feelings. This can be a great burden for a child to bear. Children need to learn how their behavior affects others, but if they think your state of mind is their impossible responsibility, they may want to emotionally take care of you, and you certainly don't want that! Guide your children with love and respect, and let them know that you will not tolerate unacceptable behavior. Do praise them and share your experience, but don't focus entirely on your feelings.

If you are lacking good communication and assertiveness skills, investigate opportunities in your area for groups or classes where you can learn and practice these essential skills. Search for self-help books on the topic of communication. Recall Jill who adopted a passive, caretaker stance early in life. Knowing how to speak up and stand up for yourself will empower you, and you will not need food as medication.

SHIFT YOUR PERSPECTIVE

As children, we ask questions. We observe the world around us, and we come to conclusions about how the world works. We learn many things, and then we incorporate much of this knowledge as our truth. Let me share an example.

As a small child, I loved breakfast. The foods served at that meal were my very favorites—french toast, orange juice, and bacon, for example. I always asked for more bacon, but as is often the case in a large family, food was rationed, and I would only receive two small pieces despite my whining and begging for more. When my mother removed the bacon from the refrigerator, she cut each slice in half. In reality, I was only getting one full strip, which was being passed off as two. Well, I was not easy to fool. I was aware of my mother's scam and even confronted her about her practice of cutting the bacon, but still, she had the power over who got what, and I never got more than my two little halves.

A few years ago, my sister and I were spending time together, and for some odd reason, our mother's practice of cutting the bacon in half came up in conversation. I told her how frustrated I had been on those mornings when I did not receive enough bacon. She smiled and listened patiently to me as I expounded upon our mother's unfairness. When I was done, my sister pointed out that it had not been a scam at all. Our mother simply cut the bacon in half because she didn't have a pan big enough to accommodate full-length slices!

My reality was completely different from my sister's. Later, I did ask my mother why she cut the bacon strips in half, and my sister was correct. She really didn't have a pan big enough to cook full slices. The lesson here is we make assumptions all through life based on our experiences and observations, and we don't always realize there are other perspectives. Our reality is, after all, our reality, and we hold fast to it. Sometimes in doing so, however, we may paralyze ourselves and remain stuck in unhealthy beliefs and the uncomfortable feelings that accompany them. So it is important to keep an open mind. Our realities can shift and change from moment to moment as we learn more and do more.

THINK POSITIVE THOUGHTS

My mother used to say, "Count your blessings, Denise," when I was playing the role of the misunderstood, unappreciated, spoiled child. I didn't like this. It was not the response I wished to receive. I recall feeling so angry with her! Obviously, when there was a valid concern, my mother would be there to care for me, but she knew the difference between the expression of my real needs and my manipulative, pouting demeanor designed to seek attention in an unhealthy way. She was on to me! "Count your blessings," she'd repeat, and I would stomp off to brood about how unfair and cruel this world could be and how I had been personally targeted to have a miserable life. (I admit I could be a bit melodramatic. Some say I still am from time to time.)

Now I can't help but smile and appreciate the wisdom of my mother's mandate to be grateful. It was not welcomed at the time, but now I recognize the immense value of my mother's words. We all have down times, and it is hard to keep our vibrational energy high and positive. Being grateful, however, can transform negative situations and feelings into positive ones. Shifting of our focus from negative to positive is central to the creation of our most joyful, healthy lives. This is why.

INTRODUCTION TO THE LAW OF ATTRACTION

We know like attracts like. This is the Universal Law of Attraction. Today we hear of this law through books such as *The Secret* by

Rhonda Byrne, a wonderful compilation of writings by many of the greatest thinkers of our past and present—Jack Canfield, John Gray, Winston Churchill, Albert Einstein, Thomas Edison, Isaac Newton, Plato, Buddha, and Alexander Graham Bell, just to name a few. It is remarkable that all of these great masters delivered the same message. All agreed that the Universal Law of Attraction exists and that we attract to ourselves that which we focus our attention on.

We can also learn how to deliberately create what we desire via the channeling by Esther Hicks of Abraham, a nonphysical group of teachers. You will learn more about the teachings of Abraham soon in the "Nurture your Creative Spirit" section. You will discover that these amazing teachings deliver the same message I am giving you here—like attracts like.

When we focus on the negative, we are affected in many ways. We attract more negative thoughts to ourselves and usually reach for unhealthy foods to ward off the negative emotions these thoughts bring. We then feel unhappy and disappointed in ourselves and feel worse, leading, of course, to stronger urges to self-medicate to get rid of the very feelings we are creating. I share the following story to illustrate:

I was sitting on the couch with my then four-year-old grandson, Timmy. We were watching a television cartoon show and laughing together. I was so content to be with him and appreciated every moment. All at once, Timmy's little face became grim and serious. He leaned over and peered closely at me. He studied my face as though he had never seen it before. "Grammy," he exclaimed, "do you know you have wrinkles?" He seemed horrified, and I must admit I did not appreciate having my sweet little grandson point this out to me. I knew I was beginning to shows signs of aging. Intellectually, I reasoned that these markers of my youth's demise represented a beautiful, graceful passage into wise womanhood. I was becoming a fifty-year-old crone, and in theory, I liked the idea.

I told Timmy that the lines he saw were not wrinkles, but instead were lines of love. Timmy thought about this for a long moment and then slowly replied, "No, Grammy, they really are wrinkles." He was so positive and matter-of-fact. I insisted they were creases of love, and he insisted they were not. As we continued to discuss my wrinkles, I began to feel sad. Deep down in my heart, I knew he was right. I was getting older, and like it or not, nothing could halt that process. The wrinkles were unquestionable evidence. I felt sad, scared, angry, and helpless all at once. So even though I knew better and have taught others to care for their emotions without resorting to food abuse for over twenty-five years, I did what I have always done under such stressful circumstances. I ate and ate and ate some more. I quickly pushed my feelings away with more than a few cookies and went on with my life. It took time to realize I was feeding myself as a way of suppressing my feelings and denying reality.

Outwardly, I appeared cavalier about my aging process. On the surface, I joked about it and laughed at Timmy's concerned observation. Deep inside, on another level, my emotions had been stirred, and I began to worry about it. Although I wasn't consciously concerned, I harbored a multitude of feelings. I was growing older—outwardly, accepting and calm; inwardly, in turmoil. I started to change. I didn't realize back then that chronological age really doesn't matter. I began to give up on things, to think of myself as old. I stopped considering myself strong and healthy and started to feel weak and helpless. I became depressed. As I noticed the changes in my body that were heralding the next stage of my life, I felt betrayed. This body that had always been so healthy and flexible was slowly changing in ways that were hard to experience and worse to watch.

I was mourning my youth and didn't realize it. I was angry, scared, helpless, and profoundly sad at times. My self-concept was altered. My self-esteem suffered. My body image changed radically in negative ways. I could not avoid this passage, but I didn't like my feelings. I did not want to face my own mortality, nor did I want to feel any of what I was experiencing. I tried to deny the existence of these painful emotions. To manage these hard times and keep my feelings in check, I ate. I ate a lot, and it worked for a while. I kept filling the body that was no longer my friend with sugar, carbohydrates, salt and fat and I gained weight— a lot!

One day it occurred to me that if I continued this uncontrolled grazing, I would just be more and more miserable. I could become a very large and unhealthy older woman, or I could blossom into an older woman who was not only healthy, but proud of herself as well. The choice was up to me. I knew instinctively that I had to exchange my negative thoughts for positive ones. I tried, failing at times and succeeding at others, and gradually (not all at once), I began to feel better.

As soon as I began to forego cookies and candy, my helplessness and fear returned with a vengeance. I had eliminated the buffer that had been protecting me from my feelings. My internal saboteur urged me to turn to my trusted friends—sugar, carbohydrates, salt and fat —to anesthetize myself again. At times, I did just that. (Remember, no one can behave perfectly every moment.) But, gradually, I began making self-loving choices more frequently and feeding myself less often. As I allowed myself to experience my emotions, a funny thing happened. I stopped overeating! My despair gradually turned to acceptance, and acceptance blossomed into self-love and appreciation.

Certainly, difficult feelings continue to creep into my experience at times. Life is like that. It just is. Some moments, and even some days, are filled with tears of sadness. Others are brimming with tears of joy. It's all part of the process of being alive. It is human nature. I do not always like it, but resisting it is harder in the long run. Allowing the feelings to exist and experiencing them paves the way to acceptance. It is helpful to remind ourselves that we need painful experiences because we determine what we *do* want by identifying what we *do not* want. The valuable times we would prefer not to have are helping us move along and clarify what we want. That's the way it works.

If we resist and try to keep our emotions tucked away, as Zoe did, chances are we will be tempted to medicate ourselves with food. We will suppress our feelings and bury them deep inside. This behavior will lead us to either the refrigerator or supermarket again and again. We will continue to seek relief and try the same ineffective remedies. We will eat and expect the eating to take care of everything, but the emotions, if not expressed, will surface repeatedly. The sugar, simple carbohydrates, salt and fat fix will only last a short time. We may profess, to ourselves and others that we wish to be healthy and fit, but unless we express our feelings, we will continue to sabotage ourselves as in the past. By the way, did I mention that the definition of *insanity* is "doing the same thing and expecting different results"?

So it is time to do something different. It is helpful to cry, keep a journal, read inspirational books, and talk with trusted friends. We can look within ourselves for answers and trust our intuition to guide us. It is most important to acknowledge our vulnerability and use the realization of our mortality to help us better appreciate each day, each moment, and each breath.

I cannot halt my aging process, but I can express my feelings about it. There are many feelings I did not enjoy and still don't. I have, however, grown to accept the changes in my body. I realize I am a work in progress and will remain so until I draw my last breath. I now periodically allow myself to grieve my fading youth and embrace each of life's challenges as natural parts of the life process. I thank little Timmy for his honest observation. His exclamation propelled me into the inevitable exploration of my own aging process. Now I can truly say the wrinkles are love lines and mean it—at least most of the time.

There are clearly defined stages of life—child to adolescent, adolescent to young adult, etc. We are constantly in transition. Each day we are different than we were the day before. Every breath transports us to a new moment in time. We are all striving for balance as we proceed along our life's path. It is tempting to anesthetize ourselves with sugar, simple carbohydrates, salt and fat to dull the feelings that accompany the stressful moments. We have learned to do this well. Each time we forego the temptation of junk food we are taking a big step closer to achieving the balance and contentment we have been striving for. We are successfully training our Appetite and creating our delicious life.

What are some of the challenges you faced as you passed from one stage of life into another? Allot yourself time to think about it. Each of us has traveled from birth to where we are right now. Each step has meant letting go of the past, embracing the present, and moving forward. We are unconsciously in mourning even though we accept the present and anticipate the future. Some stages have been easier for us than others.

Do you recall when you first realized you were leaving childhood behind? How did you know? How did you feel at the time? How did your self-concept change? Did you vacillate for a while between wanting to remain a child and wanting badly to grow up? Chances are you experienced periods of fear, doubt, and confusion. Movement through the stages of our lives inevitably stirs emotions deep within, whether we are conscious of them at the time or not. As physical changes show themselves, we need to embrace each passage. Dealing with each transition will benefit us greatly.

This may seem contradictory at times, because as you resist the temptation to medicate your feelings, you are likely to experience the discomfort you have been trying to avoid. Outwardly, this will not feel helpful to you, but inwardly, you are letting yourself know that you are equipped to manage all of your feelings. You will move through them instead of avoiding them, and you will end up in a much more calm and peaceful place. You are then working as a team with your Appetite to make decisions based on your true desires.

Once you have trained your Appetite and mastered the art of tuning in to your intuitive voice and simply living with your feelings, emotional overeating becomes a behavior of the past. You feel more energetic. The more you think positively, the better you feel, the less you seek food to soothe your feelings, and the more you find to be positive about. You are proud of yourself. Your weight stabilizes at a healthy level. You enjoy and appreciate life in ways you never have before, and you are living your delicious life!

A NOTE ABOUT BARIATRIC SURGERY

Some of you may have undergone a form of bariatric surgery to reduce the size of your stomach, thus enabling you to eat only small amounts of food at frequent intervals in order to lose weight. Those I have worked with who have had such a procedure reported that even a small amount of sugar would make them ill. So to those of you who have taken this step, or may be preparing to, please be aware that your feelings will be intensified, as you will not have the anesthetic effect of sugar, simple carbohydrates, salt and fat that you have depended upon in the past to dull them.

This situation makes your task even more urgent. It is in your best interest to read the section on expressing yourself and begin searching within yourself to identify what you are feeling, name your feelings, and then share them with others. You will have no choice but to feel difficult emotions without the relief food has offered in the past. Consider this a good thing. Your internal guidance system will be louder and clearer. Please pay attention to your feelings and go within yourself to decide how to best take care of yourself from moment to moment.

Be extra gentle with yourself while your physical and emotional bodies are catching up with and adjusting to the radical changes that surgery has produced. This is indeed a fabulous opportunity for you to get to know yourself more intimately than you have in the past and to begin serving yourself very well. Please pay close attention to what you need and make yourself number one on your list of priorities. You have taken a big step. You have made a courageous choice to have necessary, life-saving surgery. Be proud of yourself!

ADJUST YOUR ATTITUDE

Following is a brief account of an experience I had that taught me much about expectations and attitude. *When I was little I wanted everyone to treat me with unconditional love. I was, after all, a spirit of love, and I knew this. (All babies just do.) I wanted to be honored and respected and validated at all times. I was special. I was a sparkling little child. Right away, my expectations were not met. People had things to do and think about other than to simply cater to me. I didn't like this. If I wanted a hug and got a bottle instead, I wasn't satisfied. People all around me were busy. My mother was trying to live her own life and deal with her own pain. She, too, had had expectations that weren't always met. My father was working and trying to figure out how to survive and meet some of his own needs. I thought things should be happy and loving and peaceful all the time. They were not. I expected life to be easier and less complicated than it was. I still expect that at times, but it seldom is. Life is one experience upon another—some glorious, some devastating, some neutral, but definitely not what I thought it would be.*

My expectations of unconditional love pouring over me at every moment were unrealistic and naïve. As a matter of fact, one day I was mad at my parents and ran away from home. I had what I would call a "bad" attitude. I walked all the way to the next town, which was several miles away. About four in the afternoon, I began to get tired, my feet started to hurt, I was getting hungry, and I longed to be back home. I had a little bit of money, so I went to the nearest payphone and called home to ask if someone would come pick me up. I was certain that by then they would all be worried about me and had learned the lesson that my escapade was designed to teach—that they should treat me better. I still recall how surprised and hurt I felt when I called, only to discover that no one had even noticed that I was missing!

My thoughts that things should go my way and that life should always be fair were part of my own faulty thinking. Life is simply what it is—movement from one breath to the next. Being on Earth means learning from one moment to the next. It means trying to stay in balance no matter what other people do or say or what circumstances we find ourselves in. Of course, we cannot and never will be able to do this all the time, but we can learn from each experience we have. We can pay as much attention as possible to our feelings, and we can learn and grow from experiencing and observing them.

When we are daydreaming about our lives in negative ways, we are spending precious time out of focus. The clarity we seek is illusive, and having a supply of sugar, carbohydrates, salt and fat on hand helps us maintain our fuzzy thinking and mute our feelings. We become anesthetized and dull. What would we all be doing, thinking, feeling, and saying if we weren't spending so much time as non-life-experiencing zombies?

Would we be using the lessons we learn to take more risks? Would we be daring to have our own feelings and express them? Would we risk letting our children have their own points of view and feelings, and would we spend more time listening to and learning from them? Would we be facing more challenges and making changes? How would your life be different if you were facing each moment of it with courage, clarity, and conviction?

CHANGE WHAT YOU CAN, ACCEPT WHAT YOU CAN'T

In Alcoholics Anonymous participants recite a very powerful piece called *The Serenity Prayer*: "God grant me the serenity to accept the things I cannot change; courage to change the things I can; and wisdom to know the difference." Members ask their higher power to help them change the things in their lives they can, to accept those things they cannot change, and to have the wisdom to know the difference. Many of us would like to change things in our lives that can be changed, but we don't think we are capable. There are things in our lives that cannot be changed, yet we keep beating our heads against the wall stubbornly trying to change them. Why do this to ourselves?

Why are we so often discontent? Why do we attempt to do the impossible and then beat ourselves up when we are unsuccessful? Life really doesn't need to be this hard. Things get easier when we pay attention to what we feel and really listen to the messages our feelings transmit. We know if we feel good, we are making the right choices. If we feel bad, we have strayed from the path we want to be traveling.

It requires courage to change things, to truly follow your inner guidance. You may ruffle feathers when others do not approve of your actions. It is really no one else's business, but they may feel threatened when they see you becoming interested in your own life and pursuing your dreams. It is vital that you do not let the opinions and feelings of others deter you from following these dreams. After all, this is your life, and it is your responsibility to make of it what you want. In just the same way, others are responsible for their feelings and reactions, even though they may try to convince you that you are making them feel a certain way. Realistically, you are not that powerful. You can't *make* them feel anything.

To illustrate this point, if you were a client in my office and suddenly began yelling at me, telling me I am a worthless therapist, that I shouldn't have any degrees on my wall, and that I am a poor clinician, and then stormed out of my office, slamming the door behind you, I would have a reaction. I could sit there with my head in my hands and feel dreadful, believing that I am, indeed, as awful as you said I am, or I could exclaim, "Wow! I must have hit a nerve! She sure is angry!" The client's behavior is the same, but my reaction is totally different.

You see, I choose how I react. Our reactions to situations are up to us although it may not always seem that way. For example, if you were to decide to start taking art classes in the evening, your family members could respond in a negative way: "Do you have to be out at night? You are so self-centered. We really need you at home." Or they could respond in a positive manner: "Great! We're glad you're doing something for yourself. Enjoy the class. We can't wait to see your artistic creations. We support you!"

You have made your decision. You are not hurting anyone else by attending the class. You deserve to be happy, and the pursuit of your art will bring you great joy. It is up to those around you to handle their own feelings and reactions. They will adjust. Pursue your dreams. That is the only way you will be happy, and if you are not happy, you will never attain the balance, peace, and joy you are seeking. And I should mention that if you are not happy, then those around you are not likely to be happy, either.

The other side of the coin is learning to accept that which you cannot change. To explain this concept, I will use the example of a client I worked with a number of years ago. I will call her Ellen. Ellen was a quiet, gentle woman whose husband had been unfaithful. Her subdued demeanor turned to rage whenever she thought of him.

Every time she came into my office, she would immediately launch into a tirade about how horrible her ex-husband was, how badly he had hurt her, and how angry she felt.

At first, I simply listened and allowed her to vent her rage. I thought this would continue for a while and then she would stop and begin to focus on herself, but for months, Ellen's sessions were all the same—filled with poisonous venom. I finally explained to her that if we were to make progress, she would have to not only vent in her sessions, but also speak to me about herself and the other things on her mind. I encouraged her to express her anger for the first fifteen minutes of each session, and when that time was up, we would change the discussion to other things.

I adhered to this schedule for quite a while, but Ellen's rage was still the utmost concern on her mind, and I began to doubt that I could help her at all. Finally, after many more months without progress, I decided it would be in her best interest to terminate her therapy with me and refer her to someone else. This was a very difficult decision for me to make. I had grown to care about her a great deal, and it saddened me to think I could not help her. I explained to Ellen that I no longer felt her therapy was progressing and that she would need to forgive her ex-husband and accept what she could not change about her past experience in order to move on.

I pointed out that chances were good that her ex-husband was simply living his life and enjoying himself, while giving no thought to her, and meanwhile, she was continuing to harm only herself with her negative thoughts and feelings. I will never forget that day. It was as if a brilliant light bulb turned on in Ellen's mind. I could see a long, absent sparkle in her eyes. She got it! At once, she realized that accepting what had happened and forgiving him would free her to finally let go and begin enjoying her own life.

Forgiveness is for you; it is not for the other person. It does not mean that wrongs done to you are OK. They are not, and you never need to accept that they are. But having the wisdom to let go of what you cannot change—and you can never change the past—can free you to move swiftly along your path to joy and freedom. So remember the serenity prayer. It is powerful and valuable.

APPRECIATE THE PAIN

It is hard to imagine being grateful for the painful experiences you have had, isn't it? To think that someone who hurt you was also giving you the gift of a necessary, maturing experience absolutely challenges and stretches your imagination. Think of it this way for a moment. Someone hurt you, perhaps very badly. That was definitely not fair. It was unjust and unacceptable. No one should ever be harmed, and in an "ideal" world, no one ever would be. The hurt you felt as a victim may have been intense. We were all hurt in some way as children. We have all managed to find ways, albeit not always healthy, productive ones, to survive and progress into adulthood.

Now, as you look back, you may begin to see ways in which your tormenters presented you with the exact life lessons you are here to learn. Please understand that I am *not* saying it is ever acceptable to hurt another. It never is. What I *am* saying is that life is not always fair or just, and most of us have been victimized in one way or another. That is the past, and we must move on to learn and grow through our years. It is possible to appreciate our histories, especially after the experiences, and to learn and grow from the pain we have endured.

For example, if you were harshly and unjustly criticized as a child, you may now be able to understand that it was your mother or father's issue and not really about you. This may help you to not personalize others' words and behaviors too readily. Instead of reacting to what you perceive as their judgments and criticisms, you can recognize that their perceptions have little or nothing to do with you.

125

Instead, they are a reflection of their own feelings of inadequacy and doubt.

If you were abused and victimized, you were not to blame. Through this painful past, you emerged into adulthood knowing that you will never allow anyone to abuse you again. You also know what it feels like to be powerless and oppressed, and perhaps you have learned not to react to your oppression by oppressing others. These lessons are certainly not easy, and each experience of your past prepares you to face situations in your life today. Each challenge and each lesson learned moves you along your spiritual path. You get closer to the clarity, peace, and vibrancy of your soul and farther away from old, self-destructive patterns and fuzzy thinking.

You have a life, such as it is. You have a history. And you have a body in whatever condition it is in today. The question is what do you wish to do now, in the present? You can spend the rest of the time you have on this planet asleep and filled with regrets. You can anguish about the hand you were dealt. You can remain filled with bitterness and rage. If you act in this way, however, you assure that you will continue to feel depressed and anxious, and you are likely to seek food to soothe yourself. Remember that like attracts like, and your negative thoughts will only bring negative experiences and more negative thoughts.

You will be avoiding yourself, your feelings, and your life. You will sleepwalk through each day waiting for changes to happen to you, and they never will. Being fixated on the past and being a perpetual victim will keep you in a state of anxiety and reactivity, and you will never take action to make the adjustments necessary to craft your delicious life as richer and more rewarding. You can, however, turn this around by heeding the feeling messages you have trained your Appetite to deliver.

STOP AND THINK

Stop and think. What do you truly want your life to be like? What would you need to do today as a first step to creating the life you dream of and imagine? Please encourage children you know to ask the same questions. Talk with them, encourage them, and help them think as clearly as possible (at their ages) about what kind of things they love to do. Help them tap into their passions. Don't limit their dreams; ask them to expound on them. Listen attentively, and applaud their ideas (even though they may seem unrealistic or silly to you). Doing this with them will also help you get a clearer picture of precisely what you want for yourself.

Consider that your path requires you to greet the circumstances of each moment with awareness and experience each and every feeling that passes through your body. Thoughts and feelings naturally accompany every experience, and at times, they come in torrents. To truly grow, change, and fulfill your purpose on this earth, in this lifetime, you must be open to every precious feeling you experience.

Embracing painful feelings and viewing difficult experiences in a positive way is a supreme challenge. To know, in the midst of painful circumstances, that you are learning and developing in the most beautiful way requires trust in your higher purpose. You will not be able to do this perfectly every time. That is not human nature. If it were, you would not continue to grow and change. You would not learn and improve, and much of your earthly purpose would cease to exist.

When you feel butterflies in your stomach, observe this sensation. That is only your anxiety. Underlying this is always a fear that you are not lovable. YOU ARE. You can trust this! If you have children in your life, help them identify, articulate, and experience their feelings. Your job is to know that you are lovable and to teach them that they are, too. You reflect love and appreciation to them through your eyes, your words, and your actions, and they, in turn, will reflect that love and joy back to you hundredfold.

In my experience treating people with food-control problems, most, perhaps all, express disappointment with their lives and harbor self-expectations that are unrealistic. You have learned how negative self-talk originates, and you now understand the importance of changing negative attitudes and beliefs to positive ones. This is a necessary part of having healthy relationships. Evaluate the relationship you have with yourself as well as your relations with others. This will give you valuable information you can use to guide yourself and your actions in relationships in the future.

The importance of changing your attitude to manage emotional overeating is vitally important. You are learning through the stories I provide that the key to successful weight loss and its management lies in your ability to focus your attention inward in a positive way. You will be learning more about the Law of Attraction, and you will learn that it is necessary to focus your attention in positive ways to attract more positive aspects into your life. Again, remember that change must come from within.

DISCOVER YOUR POWER

Many of us often feel dull. We push down our energy when difficult emotions arise. For example, if we are tired, we reach for a snack. If we are tense and irritated, we grab handfuls of potato chips or crackers. If we feel discouraged and lonely, we head to the store for ice cream. None of this helps our situation in the long run, but as did the women and men in all of the case studies, we do it anyway—again and again and again. We learned at an early age to fix our feelings this way; however, as you may know, this is a dangerous, vicious cycle that can lead to despair. One way to break this pattern is being brave. Let me explain.

Anesthetizing ourselves with sugar, carbohydrates, salt and fat certainly makes sense if we can barely make it through our days and not feel passionate about something or not become immersed in an activity we love. But is that really all there is to life? It is up to us to create our lives. How would you begin? When was the last time you thought about it? Have you ever taken the time to truly get to know yourself? If we don't spend the time and effort to look within ourselves, life can feel pretty empty and meaningless. Then we soothe our discontented, unfulfilled selves with food, drugs, alcohol, and the like. I know there are more meaningful ways to live life, and I want to share these thoughts and ideas.

Here is a blueprint of how to begin. Eat well. Choose foods that nourish your body. Give your body the tender loving care it deserves. Give it lots of pure water, sunshine, rest, exercise, and many things to smile about. Attend to your body through massage, stretching, and breathing. Relax. Try not to take things too seriously or too personally. Challenge yourself. Take risks.

Let me use myself as an example. I have always been a worrier. I worried about everything. You name it, I have worried about it. I was in a constant state of anxiety. Suffice it to say, I arrived in my adulthood driven to take care of everyone around me. Translated, this meant I needed to control them. If I saw someone failing to do what I thought was best, I would rush to the rescue. I thought I knew what was best for everyone. I was wrong.

One day it occurred to me that taking everyone's pain away and minding other people's business might not actually be my job. If I was spending my time minding other people's business, who was minding mine? My job was to respect and love them but also validate their choices and feelings. I learned I also had to love, respect, and validate myself. This was a revelation! It seemed remarkable that I could pay attention to myself—a novel and frightening idea! I resisted because I was afraid people wouldn't love me if I wasn't hovering with concern and advice. Again, I was wrong. But how could I change?

SUMMON COURAGE

How could I, a woman in her early twenties with low self-esteem and no confidence, find what I needed to jump-start my way into a different life experience? I was an unhealthy, overweight, overworked young mother of three. How was I going to find the vitality and enthusiasm that I so badly needed for each day? How could I convert a worrier's persona into that of a "warrior"? How could I become brave? It was going to take many steps, mostly forward, but I also needed to know there would be some slipping and sliding backward in the process. I had no idea what to do.

Then I took a big risk. My kick-start and one of the first steps toward my empowerment was learning to ride an off-road motorcycle, something I had always wanted to do. (OK, call me crazy.) I placed my large derriere on top of a very fast motorcycle and challenged myself to become an off-road motorcycle racer. I didn't want to be just a woman riding a bike; I wanted to ride well, I wanted to ride fast, and ultimately, I wanted to race. The idea seemed outrageous at the onset, but as I began to ride (very slowly and cautiously at first), I discovered a whole new me hiding inside. Suddenly, the world seemed different. I felt more powerful, more adventurous, and I began to build confidence and value myself more than I imagined possible.

What might your first step be? Take stock of yourself. Do an inventory of your innermost ambitions. Use your imagination. What would you do today if there was nothing to stop you? What would you do if you could act out your secret ambition? Would you climb a mountain? Pilot an airplane? Swim, run, and bike in a triathlon? What did you love as a child? Think of what you can do to revive your spirit, to rev your inner engine. In the inspiring lyrics of the song "If I Were Brave" (©Jana Stan Tunes/English Channel Music ASCAP), co-written with Jimmy Scott, Jana Stanfield asks, "What would I do today if I were brave?" Ask yourself that question every day, take action, and watch your life change.

In my case, the thought of being on a motorcycle was preposterous. I was extremely overweight, always tired, and often depressed. I was scared and lacked confidence; however, I had this picture in my mind of flying down the woodland trails, weaving from side to side with a big smile on my face as I negotiated the twists and turns of the terrain. Most of the time, it wasn't that easy or romantic. In fact, it wasn't like that at all. My vision certainly did not match reality. I spent more time on the ground, in the mud, or under my bike than I did on top of it. I had to wear long sleeves and pants to cover my bruises. Then I noticed that each time I rode, I stayed upright a little longer than I had before. I wore tall leather boots, a belt to protect my kidneys, lots of padding, and thick gloves. Eventually, I learned how to cross railroad tracks and logs. Soon I could negotiate deep water holes without falling—at least most of the time.

Each trail, power line, or mud hole I encountered presented a new challenge. Racing became a metaphor for my life. Gradually, I was able to apply my new self-confidence to everyday challenges. Of course, I still had a long way to go. There were times when I was flying along through life with a big smile; at other times, I felt as I did before—stuck in deep mud or upside down off the trail with my bike on top of me.

As the months and years slid by, trail riding became less painful. Focusing on the trail ahead and my performance took my mind off the more difficult aspects of daily life. I began to feel more alive and less anxious and depressed. I became more confident and discovered my progress riding the trail paralleled my progress in life. I noticed I was having more fun—both on and off my motorcycle.

Surely, this was about much more than just sitting on a bike! Actually, each ride propelled me into a more positive frame of mind. As my skills on the bike improved, I felt more competent in my role as a wife, mother, daughter, and employee. I was more conscious of how I treated my body, and this led to taking better care of my mind and spirit as well. Please note I'm not saying this one act of motorcycling provided me with a magic answer or that my path was miraculously transformed into a positive, productive one. I am saying it was a start—a kick-start.

My clients often share their childhood adventures—things that took place before they learned the adult lessons of being fearful, anxious, worried, and overburdened caretakers. We discuss these stories, and often, my clients are surprised to find they, too, have a warrior hidden deep within. Many who come into my office, with or without food-control issues, find reclaiming childhood playfulness frees them to become interested and involved in the development of something new in their lives. This transformation may be apparent immediately or in more subtle changes that take longer.

Epiphanies come in their own ways and at their own times. Ask yourself what you would like to add to your personal life. Don't consider an activity because you feel you should like it or because someone makes a suggestion. Only consider things that ring true for you. Close your eyes right now and think about times you have felt joyful. Then ask yourself these questions: When were some of those times? Why did I feel so happy? What made those experiences important and freeing? Were some of these times when I took on new challenges, spent time with neighborhood friends, or enjoyed an activity by myself? What can I do today to recapture some of those illusive feelings? Make a plan to do something right now—and do it!

TAKE RISKS, BE ADVENTUROUS, AND HAVE FUN!

Who are you? Are you a painter, a skydiver, a craftsperson, or a gourmet cook? Maybe you're a deep-sea diver or a yoga instructor. It doesn't matter. What does matter is that you're having fun. Try different things. If you try something and don't like it, try something else. Get actively involved in the process of living your life consciously. Be proactive. Don't wait for life to happen, because it won't. Train your Appetite to tell you what you need. It could be more socialization, or it might be solitude. Then listen to the sage advice your feelings are transmitting through your Appetite and take appropriate action.

Only you can do it. Only you can take responsibility for making the changes you want and creating the YOU you want to be. No one else can or will do it for you. Managing your life is your job. Don't think of yourself as a human casualty. YOU ARE NOT A VICTIM! The time to act is now! Each moment that passes by without doing something for yourself is one more moment you have missed. Act now!

I certainly missed my share of opportunities along with many of the gifts life has to offer. My words are written solely to give you the impetus to create the most exciting and delicious life you can. Separate yourself from all the roles you play in life—parent, child, friend, partner, and so on—and spend time thinking of who YOU are. If I had done this, I might not have followed my path through the full spectrum of eating disorders. I might have majored in drama in college and traveled through Europe before I settled down at the ripe old age of nineteen to marry and give birth to three children in quick succession. (The truth is I felt I had to accept the first marriage proposal that came along. I thought no one else would ever ask me.

Sad.) Introspection was something I knew nothing about back then. I did not have any idea who "I" was, but in retrospect, I can see that my self-esteem level was at rock bottom.

When I ask a client, "Who are you?" I often get a teary reaction, simply because a conscious response had never been considered. Most women are far too busy attending to the tasks of daily living and the needs of everyone else to spend time getting to know themselves.

Spend time contemplating what you love to do. Brainstorm some ideas. No matter how far-fetched or impossible they seem, capture them on paper. This will grease the cogs of your brain and refresh your spirit. Feelings deep inside of you become the manifestations of your dreams. You can create something new in your life if you think about what you want. Spend time discovering who you are. Only then can you move toward the delicious life you truly want to have—filled with zest, joy, health, and balance.

Discard the worrier on the outside and uncover the warrior on the inside. As you do this, emotional overeating experiences will become fewer and farther between. Eventually, you will notice you are eating to meet your real needs—not every time, not perfectly, but most of the time. That is the goal! You and your Appetite will be able to work together easily as you craft the life plan of your dreams.

NURTURE YOUR CREATIVE SPIRIT

Children are full of energy. They are spirits in little bodies, and they are extremely creative. Just observe a toddler at play and you will see this. My children enjoyed endless hours of creative play, using their imaginations to construct towns, tents, and racetracks and to invent all sorts of imaginary activities, games, and scenes. I remember Fischer-Price dollhouses, fire stations, and farms. I particularly remember the day my tiny daughter, Mimi, decided to put her gerbil into her Fischer-Price phone booth. It was a fabulous idea on the surface, but she failed to realize that the little animal would protest against this confinement by plunging its teeth through her finger. She learned a very painful lesson from that, but she forged on undaunted by the experience to create new forms of play.

She didn't try to make the poor little gerbil part of her imaginary play any longer, but she continued to be inventive and recruited other children in the neighborhood to put on plays and shows, which she directed. She continued her creative escapades and was always coming up with something interesting and fun to do alone or with friends.

I remember wonderful days before television captured children and held them hostage, sitting spellbound and motionless while passively watching the activity outside of themselves instead of actively delving into their minds and hearts to ignite the sparks of their own creativity. That is not to say that there are no benefits to some things we may find on our televisions or computers, but many young children spend too many precious hours of their days watching mindlessly instead of thinking and acting. They are missing the joy that comes from going within to invent games and fun activities.

I was horrified one day when I took my grandson to the store to buy him a toy. He had earned the toy, and our much-anticipated outing was very special. He looked carefully at the many choices on each shelf and picked up an item here and there as he carefully considered which would be the best choice. At one point, he held up a particular truck, turned to me, and asked, "Grammy, what can this toy do for me?" Instead of wondering what he could do with this toy, he wondered how it would perform and entertain him. I thought this was quite sad.

He was, and still is, a creative, loving young man, but I'd have preferred that he purchased clay, paints, or lots of paper and crayons.

I wanted so badly for him to use his imagination and take pride in thinking for himself and constructing his own reality. Do you recall playing as a small child and using your fabulous gift of imagination? A stick could easily become a magic wand or even a gun or a sword. A cardboard box could become a vehicle, a bed for a favorite doll or pet, or when tipped on its side, a playhouse. There was no limit to its possibilities. What has happened to inventive and creative play?

Recapture your own sense of wonder, and use your imagination often. Daydream. Play. Have fun. Smile more. And, like Mimi, don't give up when things don't go exactly as you'd planned. If something goes wrong, as things sometimes do, don't get stuck there thinking of yourself or your ideas as failures. Instead, move on to other pursuits. Be less serious and more lighthearted. Be playful about it. Be creative.

WHAT'S CREATIVITY GOT TO DO WITH IT?

Your joyous and creative nature is the voice of your spirit. Perhaps you have heard people say that they are not creative. Maybe you are one of those people. If you think you are not creative, you are wrong. Believing that you are not comes from faulty messages received from others that you have taken in and assumed as your reality.

The truth is we are spiritual beings, and each of us has gifts to be appreciated and shared. Perhaps your creativity has been suppressed. You may have heard comments that your coloring was not precisely inside the lines, or maybe you chose green, purple, or brilliant orange for the hair of the characters you were coloring and were told that the colors you chose were not appropriate. Chances are you learned to abandon your urges in favor of coloring pictures that would gain approval. How sad to think that the effervescent being that you were had to conform to society's standards.

Our creative self is curious, playful, and mischievous. This *is* our spiritual self. We are glorious, joyful beings who have been swept up in the complexities of this material world and have lost touch with the magic deep within our souls. We can do something about this, and to be truly happy, we must. Think of some ways you might reignite your creative, mischievous, playful spirit. Perhaps you might explore a new area of interest, attempt a new sport, take a risk, or try out for a theater production in your area. Why not take singing lessons or learn to play a musical instrument? Join a Laughter Yoga class or a Toastmasters group. Challenge yourself to speak in public.

I spent years making excuses not to join Toastmasters. I didn't have the time, I was already a professional speaker so there would be nothing new for me to learn, and so on. The truth is I was scared. I was afraid to be judged and feared I would fail and be embarrassed speaking in front of other speakers. The reality is I did feel anxious whenever I spoke, and I often still do when I approach the platform. Now I leave my home every Friday morning at six o'clock and drive the hour to my Toastmasters meeting. I do this because participating both challenges and energizes me. It is one way I keep my creative juices flowing. What will you do to keep yourself excited, challenged, and involved in life? There are no wrong choices. If something sounds exciting, fun, and challenging, try it.

We need to rekindle our spiritual flame and recapture our essence—our joy, freedom, and playfulness—if we are to stop overeating and truly nurture ourselves. We may know this on some deep, intuitive level, but how to do so is the question. We may feel confused and disconnected from each other as well as from ourselves and our spirits. The first step is reconnection.

RECONNECT WITH YOUR SPIRIT

What do we truly need and want? What is our life's purpose? How can we access spiritual guidance to help us answer these questions?

How do we tap into the joy and beauty within and all around us? These are excellent questions to ask!

People I speak with often express a desire to unite with their spiritual essence and ask how to accomplish this connection. To heal from any compulsive behavior, to heal your body, you must attend to your spirit—to heal yourself with patience, compassion, and love. Many of us know this on a very deep and private level. It is, however, as though we see ourselves separated from our spirit by a thick veil that obscures our vision. It seems impossible to be clear, to truly appreciate and love ourselves and others, and to create our life as we want it to be—without self-abusive behaviors and critical judgments.

How do you begin? This is individual. It is private and personal, and there is no one right way. Each of us has a direct line to spiritual energy and universal love, but how we accesses that power, our life source, is unique to each of us. This is also not an event, but a process—a never-ending one at that. We do not awaken one day and say, "Oh, now I am filled with spirit! Now I am truly spiritual and connected to universal intelligence and love." Instead, we get glimmers more and more often as we develop our spiritual practice. We may be surprised to notice one day that we feel a little gentler toward ourselves and others. We may feel a bit less judgmental, less critical. This is what happens as we continue to nurture ourselves and proceed along our own spiritual path.

Each of us is special and different. We are unique. Thus each person's path will be individual. How do you follow your own spiritual path? There are as many ways as there are people on this wonderful planet. To answer this question, we will need to consider many factors. First, let's look at the two basic emotions that exist in the universe—fear and love. Think of it this way. Whenever you make a choice that leaves you feeling badly about yourself, physically depleted, anxious, scared, guilty, or angry, that's fear. You have momentarily slipped off your spiritual path and are having an experience of separation from your spiritual self. This is a painful, lonely, and frequent experience of anyone who behaves compulsively. It is an experience of disconnection.

Whenever we make a choice from a place of love, we experience an entirely different assortment of feelings that are manifestations of this love—joy, peace, contentment, pride, and love itself. It is then when we know deep inside that we have stepped back onto our spiritual path and that we are progressing in our development. Self-loving choices are spiritually enhancing, and the more we make, the better we feel, and the less compulsive, self-harming choices we will make.

Another way to help yourself and to revive your spirit is giving to others. There are many opportunities to help those less fortunate. You can donate to the charities of your choice or volunteer to work in your local soup kitchen. You can sign up through local organizations or your local hospital or church to help people in your community who need transportation to various appointments. You can shop and run errands for people who are housebound or read to people who are blind. There is no limit to the opportunities that exist for helping others. (Caution: If you fall too deeply into a caretaker role, however, this can work against you. I am not suggesting that you spend so much time doing these important things that you neglect your own needs. As always, balance is the key.) A reasonable amount of time helping others will bring you great rewards. You will feel happier, and your spirit will be joyful. You will know you are doing something wonderful for yourself, and you will be dancing along on your spiritual journey. You will be smiling and glowing, and junk food will lose its appeal.

Try this for yourself. Next time you notice the urge to reach for unhealthy snacks, ask yourself what is in your best interest. What is likely to further your spiritual development verses what will inevitably push you off your spiritual path? When you make a less-than-self-loving choice (and you will because we all do at times), observe yourself. Notice how you feel physically, emotionally, and spiritually. You will likely find yourself infused with anxiety and fear, and you may feel physically depleted. You may also experience guilt and shame and feel frustrated and defeated. Without judging, just notice this experience. It is not a mistake. There are no mistakes, only lessons. This is one of those times that help you to clearly see what you don't want in your experience. This will lead to greater clarity about what you do want to create. Observe yourself and your reactions. This memory will be a valuable lesson that helps you make a different, more self-loving choice at a future time.

Please notice just as keenly when you do make a self-loving choice. This is also a valuable learning experience. You are likely to feel proud of yourself. You will have more physical energy and will feel more lovable and more connected to yourself, your children, others, and the world in general. You will know that you are progressing along your spiritual path. You will feel love, and you will notice a distinct difference. You will proceed with lightness, feeling more confident, more balanced, and calm.

The more you stop and consider your alternatives and make your choices in the spirit of love, the more you will notice peace, lightness, and joy manifesting in your life because like does attract like. You will be in closer touch with the love all around you, and you will have more fun! That is life's purpose. It is helpful to develop your spiritual life by being as self-loving as possible and nurturing your spirit. In time, you will come to trust that you are never alone. You are always connected to your spiritual source.

Trust is central to creating your life as you want it to be. When I ask clients what they want in their lives, they often give me materialistic answers. For example, they want a better job, more money, a nicer home, or a new car. There is nothing wrong with this type of wanting. Actually, it is quite the contrary; our desires for these things serve as motivators and help us conjure up the energy we need to move forward.

This sounds easy, doesn't it? We simply figure out what it is we want, summon our energy sources, and then move steadily and quickly to achieve our goals. The better job, the more spacious home, or the shiny new sports car will be our gifts. If they do not manifest quickly, if we are not able to rapidly achieve our goals, we may fear we don't deserve to be rewarded. Instead, we might fear that we deserve to be punished. This is faulty thinking, but we may temporarily lose touch with our faith and trust in universal love. And negative feelings attract more negative feelings, remember?

When our goals are not achieved as quickly as we would like, we sometimes fail to understand that life is a series of peaks and valleys and that the process is what is most important. We all get stuck sometimes. We all face obstacles that can appear insurmountable in the moment. This is part of life. How we meet these challenges and live our lives is of paramount importance.

I know from many years of experience that when I feel stuck, my field of vision narrows, and my emotions take a nosedive. I entertain negative thoughts and feelings. At times, I become discouraged and fearful because I have lost my way and have no clear path to follow and no energy to search for a new direction. I do have faith, however, that this negative time will pass. It always does, and I will reconnect with my spirit as soon as I can. This makes the hard times easier to cope with.

In the past, I repeatedly turned to self-defeating behaviors that served only to magnify my negativity. I would choose jelly donuts instead of healthier alternatives, such as talking with a friend, exercising, reading an uplifting book, or writing my feelings in my journal. I would become more depleted physically and emotionally. I would resort to caffeine for energy and hope that tomorrow would be better somehow, but most often, tomorrow would be a repeat performance of today.

Now let's look at this cycle. I know I am not alone in this experience. Something happens. We might have no idea what the precipitant is; all we know is that we feel unhappy. At times, there is a cause we can identify, such as fighting with our significant other or running out of gas and getting stranded by the side of the road. Often, however, we don't know and don't understand why we have these uncomfortable feelings.

There are so many factors that impact our moods, including the phases of the moon, seasons of the year, or our current circumstances. Our hormones ebb and flow, and the people around us have mood fluctuations that affect us as well. We are complicated beings, and life is complex. We can spend our precious time trying to figure it all out, or we can let the feelings flow through us, pay attention to them, and take the very best possible care of ourselves, trusting that this situation and the accompanying feelings will pass.

How we handle moving through the hard times is up to us. We can sit on the couch and snuggle up to a box of cookies or a bag of chips and zone out in front of the television, or we can choose healthier, more self-loving ways to take care of ourselves and deal with our feelings as we move through them and allow them to pass.

Choosing unhealthy ways to cope, be it with food, alcohol, drugs, overspending, or any other addictive behavior, leaves us filled with shame, guilt, and remorse and compels us to repeat the negative behaviors over and over again. If I choose to park myself on the couch watching movies and munching on my favorite snacks while I wait for the pizza I ordered to arrive, I am setting myself up, and part of me knows that. My outer self may be on autopilot, recreating those old, familiar, self-destructive patterns, but my inner self (that true voice deep within) knows better. If I listen, that internal voice tells me the food and the movie are serving their purpose—to soothe and suppress my feelings and to keep me anesthetized and protected from the challenges I am currently facing.

I am *not* saying never indulge yourself with "treats" and a great movie. I *am* saying enjoy it once in a while, but don't linger there too long or too often. If you do, you will not feel very well, and you will notice that years have flown by. One day you will realize that you have become older (perhaps wider), more discouraged, tired, and apathetic. You may notice that bitterness and negativity have even become your predominant states of mind. No matter when you realize this, it is never too late to change.

What can you do instead? How can you turn this dangerous, self-destructive course around? How can you prevent yourself from falling deeply into negative patterns? How can you recover if you find yourself already entrenched in a negative situation and the accompanying negative feelings and self-defeating behaviors?

First, be gentle with yourself. It is not your fault that you struggle from time to time. We all do. The very best first step to feeling better is allowing yourself your feelings. Acknowledge them, experience them, and then move through them instead of stuffing them deep down inside with sugar, simple carbohydrates, salt and fat. You won't feel such a powerful desire to hold your feelings in or avoid them once you start expressing yourself.

Remind yourself that you are not alone. We all have "those days" when we are all thumbs and nothing seems to go our way. It is part of life, and if we accept that, we can move into positive feelings and experiences much more quickly. If we trust that everything happens for a reason and rely on our intuition, knowing that we are experiencing life's challenges as an essential part of our growth process, then we can more easily embrace all of our experiences and feelings as we move forward. We can even be grateful for the painful times, as they signify the greatest growth.

Someone once told me, "The amount of pain is commensurate with the amount of growth." I didn't appreciate the wisdom contained in these words at the time, but I do now. I have come to realize the truth of it in my own experience as well as in the thousands of stories my clients have shared over time.

In order to trust, you must have something to trust in. Some people trust in God, some in spirit or light, and others in a higher power or energy. It doesn't really matter what term you use; the word is not important. Whether you choose soul, light, energy, universal love, source, or some other label, it is all the same.

(If you think there is nothing beyond this immediate life, this particular section may not apply to you. That is OK. We are all different and have different belief systems. Choose only what fits for you as you continue to read. Some suggestions will likely resonate and offer assistance as you progress along your path. Others may not fit at all.)

Deep inside, many of us are aware that there is something greater and bigger than our physical body. We know we are part of, or connected to, something, but our mortal limitations prevent us from making sense of this on a cognitive level. So we assign a name to this life force that we are comfortable with and perhaps even conjure up an image to behold. This provides us with something to hang on to that is concrete and understandable.

Is our spirit something we can ever fully understand? I don't think so. It is personal and private. It is our very essence, our energy. We can believe in it and trust it and then turn to what we believe in for guidance and love. We all need connection, and it is there for us at all times. But when we are swaddled in negativity, we feel alone and cut off from our source.

When I find myself in my miserable, familiar, negative cocoon, the first thing I find I must do is ask for spiritual guidance and the strength I need to move through the darkness into a lighter, more joyful place. Some call this praying; others consider it meditating. I call it chatting with the universe.

How it all works is far beyond me. That it works, every time, has proven true time and time again. I trust that the universe will provide when I ask for the comfort and security I need. I am never alone and neither are you. I am certain of this, and I find great comfort in it. I am not here to thrust my belief system upon you. I am simply relating what works for me and has helped hundreds of people I have counseled.

To summarize, you are here in this lifetime, on planet Earth, attempting to be the best you can be and to craft the most wonderful life possible. You know that in order to do so you must embrace all aspects of your experience—the negative as well as the positive. When you are in a positive frame of mind, things go smoothly, and you enjoy life's ride. When things go wrong, however, it all seems to change in an instant, and your memories of the recent positive times evaporate. Instead of realizing in the moment that you are simply meeting one of life's challenges or growing experiences, you might see everything around you through a dark lens of unhappiness.

It helps to realize that life is not black and white, not all good or all bad. It is a wondrous mix of a little bit of everything—a delightful assortment of experiences and opportunities to grow through and learn from.

INCORPORATE MEDITATION

For me, it is important to stay in touch with my spiritual self as much as possible. I know deep within that I have a powerful connection to something beautiful, loving, and giving. I am loved, and I know that when I feel connected to my source. When I am not feeling connected to my spirit, life has a way of overtaking me. I get wrapped up in all the external matters of day-to-day living and forget my powerful helper, spirit, is always there for me.

When I feel alone and unloved, I punish myself. I get overcome with sadness and want to collapse and sleep away precious days. When I reconnect with my source, I feel loved. I no longer feel lonely and can approach each moment of my day with curiosity, appreciation, and enthusiasm. For me, meditation is something that I resist at times, but also something that is essential for my well-being. I have always meditated sporadically, but I had one particular experience that drove home the importance of silence and solitude. Following is the story of my Vision Quest. I share it with you to encourage you to tap in to the peace you hold in your own heart.

MY VISION QUEST

A spiritual turning point in my life was my Vision Quest. As my fiftieth birthday approached, I pondered ways to celebrate that extra-special day. After all, fifty is half of a hundred, so that milestone had to be celebrated in an unforgettable way. I thought and thought and finally decided I would spend a week at a spa. Visions of wonderful foods, massages, and relaxation danced in my head. On my way to lunch, I picked up a copy of *Spa Magazine*. I thought it would be fun to read about spas and choose the perfect place for my luxurious experience.

While browsing, I spied a tiny ad that simply read, "Vision Quests, Wilderness Transitions." I was intrigued immediately. I love the wilderness and this was by far the biggest transition birthday *ever*, so I called to find out more. I learned Wilderness Transitions was a company owned and operated by two women in the San Francisco Bay area. These two competent and spiritual women (one of whom was in her mid-nineties at the time) took people into Death Valley and guided them through a most exquisite experience.

My group members met in California several times before the dates of our quest. Because I was on the East Coast, I participated in these meetings via telephone and got to know my seven fellow "questers." Through our meetings, we learned about the flora and fauna of the desert and basic safety procedures we would need to follow during our stay in the valley. I felt excited and nervous as the day when I would join my group in California approached. After all, each of us was to spend our four days and four nights alone, with no food and only one gallon of water per day. Visions of rattlesnakes and scorpions interrupted my sleep. My friends and family tried to talk me out of the adventure.

My eldest son, Sean assured me there was no need to spend the time or money to fly out west and sit in Death Valley by myself. He offered his guest room on the second floor of his home. "I'll lock you in, Mom, turn up the heat, and I won't feed you for four days!" I laughed and thanked him for his kind suggestion but stuck to my plan and soon was on my way to join my group in California.

It is difficult to explain exactly what I experienced while out west. It was, however, a transforming encounter. Each quester chose a partner, and we helped each other find the place where we would camp. Every day I would go to a spot in between our two sites and leave a rock to let my partner know I was OK. In the afternoon, the process was reversed, and my partner would go to the same spot, see my rock, know that I was OK, and leave a rock for me to see in the morning. In this way, we checked up on each other with no personal contact. No one on earth knew where I was but my partner, and only I knew where my partner had camped. If either of us arrived at our meeting place and there was no rock from the other, we would immediately go to their site to see what had gone wrong.

On the morning we were to begin, we each hiked out to our sites and set up camp. It took about two minutes to pitch my tent. Then I sat on a rock, and it hit me that I would be sitting there for the next four days. I wouldn't be preparing food or eating. I wouldn't be watching TV or listening to music. I would simply be there. I would simply *be*.

After a brief moment when I thought perhaps I should have taken my son Sean up on his offer, I settled in to experience the beauty and drama of this amazing part of the world. At first, the desert landscape seemed sparse and everything looked dead and brown. I thought it was a poor choice of environments in which to relax and appreciate nature. How wrong I was! The desert was, in fact, teeming with life.

I had visits from tarantulas and scorpions, but instead of being afraid, as I had expected, I rather enjoyed their company. (Call me crazy, but it felt very safe there, and my sense was they simply wanted to say hello.) Every night I was entertained by a little fuzzy bunny that hopped about, peeking at me from time to time to see if I had brought any food for her. Of course, I had no food, but she came faithfully every night anyway. Imagine that! Someone wants you to give him or her food, but you say no day after day, yet they're still loyal to you!

My most frequent guests were lizards that have the ability to remain completely motionless for hours as they sun themselves. Back home, I would never have had the time to enjoy them, but on my Vision Quest, time was irrelevant. I could sit for hours and feel the entire, delicious sunrise climbing slowly up my back. I could start watching the sunset at noon and remain until the sky turned inkẏ black, studded with billions of stars—a brilliant canopy of diamonds! What a spectacular show!

If I allot twenty minutes in the morning to close my eyes and breathe deeply, I can revisit my campsite in Death Valley and re-experience the peaceful nature of that setting and the calmness I felt while I was there. I can visualize the mountains in the distance, feel the warmth of the sunshine, and even smell the clean, intoxicating smells that can only exist in the desert. I can relive my quest and once again bring myself into a state of calm and appreciation.

If, when I practice my daily meditation, I ask my spirit to help me remain appreciative and treat myself and all those around me with gentle compassion and love, my day is entirely different from the days when I neglect my time of connection with the spiritual energy all around and inside of me.

Early this morning, for example, I awoke lying in bed with my head packed full of worries. The more I tried to quiet my mind, the more negative chatter I experienced. I felt tired, lonely, and unlovable. I didn't want to lie there feeling so badly, and I didn't want to get up and face another day of responsibilities and stress, either. In years past, I might have turned to food for solace. No, not I *might* have, I *would* have. I'd have chosen muffins or donuts or tortillas with butter and jam. These reliable friends would unfailingly be there to calm my frazzled nerves and soothe my aching heart. Now I know better (even though once in a while I admit I still ignore my wise self and I do succumb) and you do, too. We all know these foods will only make whatever we are feeling bad about feel worse in the long run. Most of the time we can make the more self-loving choice.

So, nearly every day, I put my feet on the floor and force myself out from under my warm, cozy covers. I position myself in my meditation chair, close my eyes, and focus on my breath. At first, my mind jumps around like a monkey, and intrusive thoughts interfere with my quiet time. I gently nudge my mind back to the present and repeatedly refocus on the sound and feeling of my breath entering and exiting my body. After a while, I began to feel peaceful and calm. My energy level rises, and my mood improves. I felt better equipped to face the challenges my day will surely bring.

For me, meditation provides a better alternative to the sugar, carbohydrates, salt and fat of bygone days. Taking twenty minutes to sit quietly and comfortably with my eyes closed, focusing on my breathing—deeply at first, then slowly, quietly, and peacefully as I continue—both centers and calms me. I choose a word such as peace or love to repeat over and over with each breath to help my mind clear itself of some of the rumbling, negative chatter. Sometimes I quietly count my inhalations and exhalations. At other times, I pray and ask my spirit to help me through the day, and when I do this, I feel a shift inside myself. I no longer feel alone, discouraged, or bombarded with negative thoughts. When I open my eyes, my energy is different, and I feel ready for the wonders of the day ahead, not exhausted and apprehensive as I had been feeling.

This is what works for me. Yes, there are days when I am unable to relax and enter a meditative state, and those days are more difficult. When that happens, I do my best to take care of myself (with varying degrees of success). I count my blessings, take deep breaths whenever I think of it, and engage in activities and conversations that are pleasant and positive.

It is always my choice how I approach my day. I can drag myself out of bed and unconsciously perform the routine duties before me. I can plod mindlessly along like a robot, and for me, this assures I will struggle and things will seem more overwhelming and stressful than they need to be. Or I can remind myself that I am a human being and, as such, cannot do everything perfectly every minute. I can approach each day as a new start and spend those few quiet minutes in the morning connecting with my spirit to remind myself of my many blessings. I can ask God to help me live this day fully, appreciating all I have and making the most of each moment. The difference between doing this or being mindless and negative is like night and day.

An unconscious, disconnected day is likely to be filled with negative experiences and emotions, many of which will scream to be soothed with food. We have all learned through experience that our old friend, food, will never fail to soothe and satisfy us in the short term.

A conscious, connected day is entirely different. Those few valuable, meditative moments can mean the difference between feeling frustrated, exhausted, and depressed or feeling peaceful, joyful, and optimistic. It is always your choice (although it may not always feel that way). Making the choices that you know are in your own best interests is not always easy. If you are feeling badly about yourself, guilty, or ashamed, for example, the last thing you want to do is treat yourself lovingly. You are much more likely to want to punish yourself with yet another day of unhealthy food and frustration. How will you turn this negative cycle around? What works for you?

CREATE SPIRITUAL SPACE

Another important step to rediscovering your spiritual/creative self is to make a space for yourself that feels cozy and conducive to relaxation. This place may be a corner in your bedroom or a room of your own. It doesn't have to be large, richly furnished, or filled with expensive things. But it has to reflect your personality. It could just be a comfy chair in a corner where you can retreat from the pressures of the world for a few minutes of quiet every now and then. If you wish your internal environment to be relaxed and peaceful, then your external environment must reflect that as well. Perhaps you can relate to my experience.

For me, silence and order are precious and absolutely necessary! Recently, I was thinking about how much I enjoy a certain sense of order in my life. I require this to relax. I don't mean that I require a sterile environment or one where every inch of space is organized, but I do feel better when I spend most of my time in places that are clean and basically neat.

As a child, I remember letting dirty clothes, discarded papers, and belongings collect in my room until my mother would finally intervene. She did not appreciate the litter, and she would offer me the choice to clean my room and be permitted to go out or not clean it and have to stay in. Obviously, under pressure, I would opt to clean my room. I would inevitably feel great once the task was completed and my space was in order. My room had been transformed into a haven in which to relax instead of a place to step over things, sleep, and search for clean clothes to wear.

In my life today, I notice the difference when my space is being managed and how I feel when it is not. By "managed," I mean the condition of my home, office, and car when I pay attention to them rather than when I ignore them and allow litter and dirt to accumulate. If I have been exceptionally busy and these areas are cluttered, I can easily feel overwhelmed. Disorganization zaps my energy and spawns out-of-control feelings. These feelings, as I know, are likely to drive me toward sugar, simple carbohydrates, salt and fat. These treats are more enticing than the vacuum cleaner or dust rags.

When you feel disorganized, out of control, and tired, your cravings will be masked as hunger. These are not really about physical hunger; they are signs that you are not content in some way. The cravings themselves are real, but they are not indications of true, physical hunger. They are messages from your friend, your Appetite, about your need for another kind of nourishment. They are about spiritual hunger. Chances are good that it is not food you are seeking; it is love. It is spiritual love and connection to your higher self that you crave. We all have these cravings, or longings, whether we are conscious of them or not. We all need to feel cared about. We need to be recognized, valued, validated, and appreciated.

Now, let's tie all this together. I am *not* saying that if you don't clean your room you are destined to feel unhappy and binge on huge helpings of chocolate cake. What I *am* saying is that to truly connect with your spirit it is helpful to create the optimal environment for yourself. When you feel peaceful in a setting, you are more likely to relax and feel the peace and tranquility within yourself. Food is less important when you feel spiritually connected and calm.

Most places of worship are quiet and simply furnished. Have you ever sat alone in a quiet chapel, mosque, synagogue, or church and felt the peacefulness? There is no mess, no chaos. There are no intrusions into your energy field. This is one reason why members of religious orders generally live in simple rooms, perhaps with only a small bed, chair, and bureau. The less clutter we surround ourselves with, the more we free ourselves to be open to universal love. Our internal state is reflected in our environment. When we exist amidst chaos, we are likely to feel chaotic inside as well. Then, of course, we will naturally head for the kitchen to examine the contents of the refrigerator once again, as if we will discover something that wasn't there when we last checked.

FENG SHUI

In the past several years, many people have become familiar with the Chinese art of Feng Shui (pronounced "fung shway"), and there are many excellent books now available on this topic. Feng Shui is a useful system for enhancing our lives and our spiritual connection as well. A life force, or energy, known as Chi (pronounced "chee") flows all around us. By arranging our homes and work and play areas in specific ways, we optimize the flow of this positive, vital life force. This reorganization of Chi creates more relaxing and energized spaces in our various environments.

One basic premise of Feng Shui is releasing extraneous things from our lives to make room for the new. Letting go of old habits, clutter, negative attitudes, and beliefs makes space for new, more productive thoughts and behaviors. We can keep this principle in mind, and as we bring more Chi into our living areas, we create more room for personal growth and increased energy in our own lives.

EXPLORE SPIRITUAL RESOURCES

Before I continue, I want to acquaint you with Abraham-Hicks, the second amazing, life-transforming resource I mentioned in "Make Friends with Your Feelings." Abraham is a group, not a single entity, of spiritual guides who speak to us about the specifics of the Law of Attraction through a woman named Esther Hicks. If you have not personally experienced or heard of channeling in the past, you are most likely skeptical, as well you should be. I encourage you to keep an open mind and visit www.abraham-hicks.com to investigate the phenomenon of Abraham's teachings for yourself. Then see what you think. If they have no value for you, that is fine. Move on. For thousands of people, however, these teachings are helping them transform their negative, painful lives to delicious lives filled with balance and joy. For many, they reveal a path from the insanity and frustration of failed weight loss efforts to one of quiet positive progress in a healthy direction.

For some, this talk of spirits and guides may be a stretch, but if you are open to the idea of spiritual guidance, as I am, this will propel you along your journey. What is so wonderful to me is that the messages of Abraham also match the messages of the great thinker's quoted in Rhonda Byrnes's book, *The Secret* (www.thesecret. tv.com). Once again, the message, or secret, is that like attracts like in our universe. This is also a primary message of this book. (You may have noticed this.) What you think about is what you draw into your life, and the Law of Attraction is as real and reliable as is the Law of Gravity.

You are the creator and simultaneously the product of your creation. You construct your reality with your thought and draw things to yourself through positive emotions, or vibrations. If you expect the best, you will get it. If you expect the worst, you will attract that. The universe does not distinguish between "good" or "bad"; it just delivers whatever matches your feeling or vibration. Like attracts like, and so it is. I have witnessed and personally experienced this many times.

But don't take my word for it, try it yourself. The next time you go out shopping at a crowded mall, for example, ask the universe to provide a parking spot for you close to the entrance. Smile and feel assured that your space will be waiting for you. Then see what happens. Your parking spot will appear just as you requested 95 percent of the time. Also, see what happens if you insist that no parking place will be vacant. That will most always be the case. You see, you are the creator—of parking spots, health, fantastic relationships, of everything. Practicing manifesting parking spaces is one way to help you build confidence in the awesome power of the Law of Attraction.

Not to be redundant, but it does bear repeating that what we think about is what we attract. So if we are thinking, "I am fat, and I need to lose weight," the universe hears that, responds to our negative thoughts (and our negative vibrational state), and keeps us feeling fat and needing to lose weight, which we have not seemed to be able to lose in the past, despite all our most sincere efforts. When we give thought to something, we invite it into our life. So could weight loss be really as simple as changing our thought patterns? Yes, I believe it can, and in fact, I believe weight loss is possible by shifting our thoughts to a positive vibration whenever possible.

One other resource I would like to mention is Jack Canfield's book, *The Success Principles: How to Get from Where You Are to Where You Want to Be.* I have never seen a more complete, step-by-step guide to creating the life of your dreams. You would do yourself a magnificent favor by checking it out. It serves as a great companion book to this one.

How can you use this wonderful information to your best advantage? You can begin by ceasing to beat yourself up. It never helps. As I emphasize so strongly in my earlier book on emotional eating, *The Taming of the Chew*, focus on the positive things about your body instead of putting yourself down or punishing yourself for so-called "bad" overeating behavior. Think about how fortunate you are that your body can serve you in the marvelous ways that it does. Appreciate yourself! Think of joyful things, and have more fun. Any positive, happy thoughts will raise your positive vibration and enable you to transform not just your physical body, but your emotional and energetic bodies as well. You will certainly be changing your life. You will be radiating positive energy!

The effects of positive thinking are powerful and magical. Of course, there is much to know about the Universal Law of Attraction that can help you—much, much more than I could possibly share in this brief chapter. So please visit Abraham's website and read and listen for yourself. I think you will be most pleasantly surprised. Invite more joy, balance, and peace into your life. You deserve this!

We are here to have fun and experience all the love and joy in the universe. We cannot do this if we are spending our precious time beating ourselves up and paying attention to all the things we perceive as "bad" or "wrong" about our lives and our bodies. Again, if we persist in saying "I am fat," for example, the Law of Attraction assures us that we will remain in a state of feeling and being fat. If, instead, we focus on the fabulous things about our bodies and visualize ourselves as healthy and slender, we feel more positive, raise our positive vibrational energy, and move steadily closer to that vision of ourselves.

According to the Law of Attraction, we can have anything. We can do anything, and we can be anything we want. We manifest our desires with our thoughts, visions, words, and feelings. We are the creators. We get what we think about and manifest our intentions. Begin to notice what messages you give yourself. Transform negative into positive. When you catch yourself criticizing yourself, stop and consider what you are doing and then shift the focus of your attention to something positive. The more you do this, the better you will feel, and the more you will find to be positive about. Your well-trained Appetite will help you along with clear, encouraging messages every step of the way.

SOOTHE AND BALANCE YOUR EMOTIONS

You may have heard life described as an emotional roller coaster, and most, if not all, of us have experienced that at times. A roller coaster moves very slowly at first as it works its way uphill. Then just when you least expect it (especially if you have shut your eyes in fear as I do when I have a lapse in judgment and allow someone to convince me to ride), it plunges downward at breakneck speed. This is all out of your control, and the experience can be either exhilarating or paralyzing. The reaction depends upon the person and his or her expectation and attitude toward the ride.

Life is similar. We move along at varying speeds and often feel out of control as unforeseen events occur. Things might be moving along nicely when, out of nowhere, something surprises us, and we plunge downward at breakneck speed. In a flash, our emotions can shift from pleased, satisfied, and relaxed to tense, angry, fearful, or hurt. Feelings may cascade tumultuously over and through us, and we are likely to feel out of control and helpless. We become victims of our feelings and succumb to their unpleasantness. Our anxiety mounts because we have no idea where the feelings came from.

It is not uncommon to ride many emotional roller coasters in a single day. We receive loving words from our partner or spouse and are filled with warmth, only to be chastised later by our boss and plunged into helplessness, shame, and anger. From one moment to the next, our feelings soar and plummet like huge waves as they rush toward the shore. We may smile one minute and sob the next.

The variety of experience and emotion is what makes life interesting, but sometimes it is hard to keep our heads above water when we are swept up in a deluge of contradictory feelings. Instead, we find ourselves tumbled by the current and unable to find the sure footing we need to support ourselves. At such times, it is important to breathe deeply and use our skills to balance our emotions. Following are a few suggestions to help.

To review, you already know ways to help yourself physically. You know that eating nutritious foods in reasonable amounts will help you feel better and more energetic. You know that the food industry has been victimizing you, and you no longer allow that. You know intuitively that your body craves clear water, sunshine, and some exercise. You have no doubt you need to relax and rest. Your body tells you what it needs, and you know your job is to care for it by paying attention to the messages it is continually sending you and then following through and giving yourself what you truly need.

Emotionally, you know what you need when you pause and pay attention to your internal guidance system—the messages from your Appetite, your feelings. You may need to cry, laugh, or have some fun. Maybe you're bored and need to engage in an interesting new activity. You might be lonely and craving company or feel anxious and need quiet time to reflect and regroup. As you pay close attention to the messages you are receiving via your emotions, you become better equipped to give yourself precisely what you need at any time.

Once you are able to stay tuned to your physical and emotional needs, you will be able to choose what you want. Most assuredly, this will help in your quest to manifest perfect health and your ideal weight. You won't be grabbing for donuts or chips when you're tired or stuffing yourself with pasta when you know you are really angry.

Of course, as you read this you are probably thinking it is much easier said than done. You are absolutely correct! For example, it is one thing to recognize you feel depressed and quite another to take the necessary action to alleviate your heavy, sad, tired feeling. Sometimes you may have no idea how to improve your mood, and because you are accustomed to soothing your discomfort with chocolate bars, you race to the candy machine to find the sweet relief you know you can count on.

You know the sugar, simple carbohydrates, salt and fat you are reaching for will only make you feel better momentarily and that, in a short while, you are likely to feel fat, guilty, and ashamed and crave more treats, which will only serve to continue the discouraging, frustrating cycle of feeling bad, eating more, feeling worse, eating more, gaining weight, feeling discouraged, eating more, and so on. This cycle leads to increased anxiety, depression, weight gain, and a multitude of physical problems associated with obesity.

Most of us have experienced this negative cycle at some point in our lives. (Personally, I have on countless occasions.) At times, we may feel like a gerbil on a wheel, running incessantly, getting nowhere, and trying more and more desperately to figure out how to stop the terrible cycle and get off of the wheel.

You may break the cycle by focusing on the present moment, being appreciative of the positive aspects of your life, or shifting the focus of your attention to something else, something happier and more pleasant to ponder. These things aid our return to balance. In addition, Bach® Original Flower Remedies can help. I use them myself and often suggest them to clients. I have seen life-changing results!

There are many alternative ways to take care of our emotions—acupuncture, polarity therapy, and Reiki, just to name a few. These work to open and balance the energy channels in our body and can help us when we have strayed from our path and feel difficult, negative feelings. Using Bach® Flowers is another alternative method of emotional healing that I especially like. To help you understand what they are, I will give you a little history and some basic instructions.

BACH® ORIGINAL FLOWER REMEDIES

Dr. Edward Bach lived in London, England, from 1886 to1936. He was a sensitive and brilliant physician who concerned himself with finding ways to help people feel better and enjoy their lives more. He believed to heal ourselves physically and emotionally, we must first heal our very life force. I agree with Dr. Bach and have seen evidence of this in my own life as well as through the experiences of clients as they have traveled their own life journeys.

My goal is not to convince you of this. (As always, I urge you to take what works for you and disregard anything that does not fit into your belief system.) It seems evident there is more to us than just the physical bodies we inhabit, this "other" part we call by many names—soul, god, light, energy, or higher power, for example. This is the part of us we cannot see with our eyes, but we know in our hearts exists and keeps us connected to source energy. This ethereal energy body needs attending to just as our physical and visible parts do. If we are truly going to heal and feel as joyful as we are meant to feel, we need to correct our negative emotional patterns and transform them into positive ones. This helps us come into emotional balance and heals our soul.

Dr. Bach also believed that before we can heal our physical bodies, we must heal our very essence, our energy. He wanted to find a natural way for people to do this and discovered the potent power of thirty-eight different flower remedies and a few blended ones made from flowers he picked from his own gardens in Mont Vernon, England.

I will mention three helpful Bach® Flower offerings here: Rescue Remedy, Rescue Sleep, and the Emotional Eating Support Kit.[1]

RESCUE REMEDY

If you are in crisis or just having a difficult time, the Bach® flower blend known as Rescue Remedy can help you. I always carry a small bottle with me to use any time I feel stressed or anticipate stress will accompany an activity in which I am about to engage. To illustrate the power of Rescue Remedy, I share the following brief, but frightening story.

Recently, Sapphi, my little therapy dog, and I were headed to our office in town. It was seven fifteen in the morning, and we had our first client coming at eight o'clock. I mused to myself about how peaceful and magnificent the day was. I felt calm and blessed as I noticed the brilliant landscape. Sunshine bounced off a brand new snowfall, and the town looked like a perfectly painted fairyland. With this attitude of contentment and appreciation, I pulled in behind my office building and parked my Mini Cooper. Little did I know that this quiet contentment would be replaced momentarily with terror.

---

[1] Be aware that these tinctures each contain 27 percent alcohol to help preserve freshness. If you are taking antibuse or are unable to take even a tiny bit of alcohol, you can put the drops in hot water or a hot drink to allow the alcohol to dissipate before ingesting. You can also request non-alcohol remedies from the Nelsons USA website.

My office building is very old, so old that the Republican Party was first formed there. In the back entrance, on the basement level, is a small vestibule with a call button to summon the ancient elevator. Once inside this tiny elevator, the door quickly slams shut. On this particular morning, I had my hands full of books and bags that I was bringing up to my office, and just as the door closed, I spotted my little dog, Sapphi out of the corner of my eye. She was still in the vestibule sniffing something, which to her was of great importance.

My office is on the third floor. I had already pushed the button, and the elevator began its ascent. I had Sapphi's leash in my hand, but the other end was still attached to her neck! She was in a perfect position to choke to death, and I simultaneously went into panic mode and autopilot. Fortunately, I knew where the toggle switch was that would shut off the power, and I hit it before the elevator had reached the first floor. Her leash was a retractable one, and I frantically dumped out the contents of my purse, grabbed my nail clippers, and cut the nylon line. Now I was trapped in the elevator with no way to know how Sapphi was! I trembled at the thought that my precious pet was in mortal danger. I pushed the down button trying to get the elevator to disregard my previous instruction to go up to the third floor, but once it had received that command, it would not disregard it and reverse direction. My heart was pounding. I was in a panic mode, and my body flooded with the stress hormone cortisol.

There was an ancient telephone on the elevator wall. I was shaking so hard that I had to hold my right hand with my left to place my fingers in the proper holes to dial 911 on the elevator's rotary phone. I got a recording on my first try and had to dial again. After a few agonizing minutes, I was given the number for my local police station. Somehow I was able to memorize it and call the station. In a tearful, loud, and shaky voice I begged the police to hurry to the back of my building to free Sapphi from her collar.

To make a very long story short, the police responded immediately, as did the rescue squad and fire department, complete with hook and ladder. They yelled up the elevator shaft that they had my dog and that she was OK. They had detached her leash. After going agonizingly slowly all the way up to the third floor, I came back down to the ground floor. When the doors opened, Sapphi was sitting there quietly surrounded by her rescue crew. I thanked them profusely, and Sapphi and I resumed our trip upstairs to the office.

Once we were safe inside, I burst into tears and hugged her tightly to my chest. She and I were both shaken and upset. It was hard to imagine being able to sit still and be truly present for my eight o'clock client who was arriving momentarily, but Sapphi and I had our jobs to do. I reached for my bottle of Rescue Remedy, put a few drops into my mouth, and gave Sapphi a few drops as well. Within moments, we both calmed down and were able to receive our client and begin our session. Sapphi nestled on my lap leaned against my chest and promptly fell asleep. That is how powerful Rescue Remedy is! I will tell you more about Sapphi in the following section on connecting with our pets.

If I am in a social situation and begin to feel anxious or fearful, I can place a few drops of Rescue Remedy on my tongue and instantly feel less nervous. (Caution: If you are using Rescue Remedy or any remedy before an important job interview or an important talk with someone, be aware of the slight alcohol content. If you will be in close proximity to another person, you may want to use a breath mint before the event. Or you can take your remedy in a hot beverage to allow the alcohol to dissipate.)

RESCUE SLEEP

Rescue Sleep is a combination of the remedies found in Rescue Remedy along with the remedy White Chestnut, which is known to quiet the mind. It is referred to as a "lullaby in a bottle" and will help you relax into a peaceful slumber. It is effective, and because sleep disruption causes us to produce excess ghrelin (the hunger hormone that also lowers the amount of calories you can burn) and reduced leptin (the satiation hormone), a good night's sleep helps with appetite regulation and healthy eating. As your quality of sleep improves, your hormones will come into balance and your appetite won't be so ravenous.

Next I will take a minute to explain three Bach® Remedies that come as a kit and directly address the problem of emotional eating.

THE EMOTIONAL EATING SUPPORT KIT

In 2008, I conducted a small, informal six-week experiment. I recruited twelve adult participants who reported they were having trouble with emotional eating difficulties. The purpose of this small study was to determine whether (or not) three specific Bach® Flower Remedies (Cherry Plum, Chestnut Bud, and Crab Apple) would help participants stop or noticeably reduce incidents of emotional overeating. Eight women and four men responded to my ad in the newspaper and expressed their interest in participating in this innovative project and trying the three chosen remedies.

Participants were first screened by telephone to determine whether they had been struggling with overeating issues, found it difficult to express their emotions, viewed their body as unattractive, and ate for emotional reasons. I then conducted a second screening to rule out participants who had ever been hospitalized with an eating disorder, had a serious psychological disorder, had ever been suicidal, or were actively bulimic or anorexic.

Volunteers met with me biweekly for a total time period of eight weeks. Each was instructed to place two drops of each flower remedy in his or her mouth or in a glass of water to sip four times per day, or as needed.

The three remedies used in the study were chosen because of the anticipated assistance they would offer participants in dealing with the most common emotions that contribute to emotional eating:

Cherry Plum allows you to stay in calm control, even when you feel like grabbing a second (or third) serving of extra cookies.

Crab Apple is known as the cleansing remedy and helps you feel better about yourself and your body, especially when you feel embarrassed by your tight clothes or disgusted over how you have misused food in the past.

Chestnut Bud helps you change negative behavior patterns and makes you more self-observant so you can notice what changes you need to make to break the cycle of overeating and dieting for good.

At each meeting, participants were asked to relate the experiences they had had during the previous two weeks, and salient quotes were captured. Following is a small sampling of quotes from participants:

- "I'm amazed! I don't feel critical of myself."

- "I'm not blaming myself any more. I have a different outlook."

- "I could get into pants this week I hadn't been able to get into in years."

- "I'm doing it. I've had no problems. I'm surprised because I don't stick to things. I'm usually so resistant to taking anything that helps me."

- "When I overate, I observed it but didn't judge or beat myself up and didn't fear I'd continue eating more."

- "I've still had no chocolate! It's so interesting…and no more night eating!"

- "This is helping me settle into a new habit. My body size isn't such a big deal."

Overall, participants expressed a dramatic decrease in episodes of overeating. They were less critical of themselves, their eating behaviors, and their bodies. Participants all agreed that the drops had helped them develop healthier habits and treat their bodies with respect, choosing healthy foods more often. It was remarkable that all twelve participants expressed many of the same feelings and experiences.

All agreed that the drops helped them decrease or stop the incidents of emotional eating. All were more thoughtful about food choices than they had been at the start and did not fear eating in an out-of-control fashion as they had initially. Participants mentioned that they were more respectful and tolerant of themselves and experienced greater appreciation for their bodies and for their lives in general.

I administered a self-rating scale during each meeting to meas-ure the extent to which each participant considered emotional eating an issue. Participants were asked at each meeting to subjec-tively rate the extent of their emotional eating difficulties on a scale of one to ten, with one being no problem at all and ten being that emotional eating is a severe, constant problem. At the beginning of the six-week study, the average value assigned to the difficulties experiences was eight and a half or above. At the conclusion, all participants rated their difficulty with emotional eating between zero (no difficulty at all) and two. Although this was a tiny study, it produced amazing results.

We already know that despite our best efforts to self-soothe in healthy ways, we can still find ourselves seeking our own "food cure" at times. These little tinctures can curb that tendency. Instead of reaching for the nearest brownie or pizza slice, you can reach for your tinctures instead. I suggest you give them a try. These are enormously helpful for most people, and I hope they will become useful and effective tools for you.

These tinctures are powerful. Once my neighbor's husband was suffering from insomnia, so I gave her a sample of Rescue Sleep for him to take at bedtime. Since she was complaining of low energy and frequent spells of exhaustion, I gave her some samples of the remedy Olive to raise her energy level. That night when it was time for the couple to retire, my neighbor's wife confused the two products and gave her husband the remedy to awaken his energy, and she took the one to make her more relaxed and tired. Needless to say, her husband was more than a little annoyed! This provides "backward" proof of the effectiveness of Bach® Remedies!

CONNECT WITH YOUR PETS

For many of us, another avenue to rediscovering our creative spirits is through a connection with our pets. You may be wondering what animals have to do with stopping emotional overeating. Plenty! As mentioned earlier, anyone with food-control issues will most likely also experience low self-esteem, elevated stress levels, physical and emotional problems, inactivity and fatigue, low self-confidence, and sometimes, social isolation. So I cannot resist including this small section on the therapeutic effects of our little furry, scaled, or feathered friends. Research has shown that living with and caring for animals helps remedy all of the above named conditions. About twenty-five years ago professionals began using animals to help patients with physical and psychological problems, and over time, the field of study has expanded. It is now well accepted that our animal friends provide us with numerous benefits. Being with them is not only good for us, but perhaps necessary for optimal health and happiness.

Many kinds of animals have helped humans in ways we are only beginning to understand and appreciate. There is evidence that people who have pets are healthier, less prone to hypertension and heart disease, have lower blood pressure, less anxiety, and manage their stress more effectively. They are more active, social, connected, and responsible and have higher levels of self-esteem. Pets give unconditional love and help us focus outside of ourselves. There is no doubt that animals of many species can help us correct imbalances in our bodily systems and, ultimately, heal eating difficulties.

Blood pressure is lowered when we watch fish swim lazily in an aquarium or when we talk with our bird, hamster, ferret, goat, or turtle companion. Petting an animal—be it a dog, cat, guinea pig, or horse—can have the same effect. Pets also provide a sympathetic ear, and we can confide our most secret thoughts and feelings without fear of being judged or exposed. This is most therapeutic! An animal provides a channel for communication, and we can express our feelings through verbal and physical interactions with our trusted pets. They provide a willing ear and are a source of unconditional love and companionship.

Sapphi

I have a West Highland Terrier named Sapphi (pronounced "Saffy"). People laugh when I tell them she is one of my greatest teachers. I'm not joking. My puppy has been sharing her boundless wisdom with me for over twelve years. I have felt blessed every day that she has occupied a place in my home and heart. Sapphi lights up when I enter the room, and I beam whenever I see her. She generously provides the unconditional love and attention I have always craved. She is my daily companion, my playmate, my confidante, and my comforter. She is vital and alive and a constant reminder of what's important in my life.

Sapphi is also a role model. She lives a simple life. Her needs are minimal. She is happy giving kisses and receiving a small bowl of crunchy food, a walk, and a few pats in exchange. This reminds me that life needn't be so complicated and serious. She doesn't need *things* to be satisfied. On the other hand, she exuberantly loves a new bone or chew toy. She enthusiastically bounces all over the room, rolls on the floor, and spins in circles when she is the recipient of such good fortune. She is wrapped in the wonder of her experience and launches her whole self into it. When there is no surprise, however, she is content with the simple routine of her life.

Sapphi is nearly thirteen years old at this time, yet she acts just as she did when she was a puppy. No one ever told her to grow up and act her age. Did anyone ever tell you that? You know you don't have to. Age is a relative term, and we truly are as young as we feel.

STAY IN THE MOMENT

Sapphi lives in the present moment, and that is one of the most important lessons she has to teach. When she is running, she is running. When she is eating, she is eating. It is that simple. If only it could be that easy for each of us! Sapphi doesn't worry about what happened yesterday, and I doubt she is concerned about tomorrow. To me, she serves as a constant reminder to be in the present moment and fully enjoy each new experience.

"Be in the moment." This phrase is something we hear quite a lot as we read much of today's spiritual literature. Many women tell me they would love to practice being in the present but have no idea what that really means, much less how to accomplish it. So I will share a few thoughts about this with you. Our minds are as busy as little monkeys swinging from limb to limb, chattering all the while about what has happened or what will happen. Seldom do we take the time to quiet this chatter and tune in to what we are experiencing in the present. Meditation, as I mentioned in "Nurture Your Creative Spirit," is so beneficial that I will address it briefly again here.

You do not need to sit in meditation for long periods of time each day trying to empty your mind and focus on your breath. It is worthwhile, however, to sit quietly on a daily basis to relax and become more mindful, but please know that it is not common to sit with an empty mind. There are persistent thoughts passing through our brains at a rapid-fire rate. We are accustomed to that. We are busy people, and we have trained ourselves to be excellent thinkers.

What we can do is allow thoughts to pass by, like fluffy white clouds moving past in the sky, and gently guide our awareness back to our breathing. Some days we may experience glimpses of the peace that is found in the slight pause between exhalations and inhalations. We may feel our heart beating and the relaxation that comes with being attuned to our breath entering and exiting our body. On other days, we may find ourselves becoming impatient. After all, we are used to working hard, aren't we? We want to be perfect and do everything perfectly. Our idea then is that we need to be actively doing, making the relaxation happen instead of passively allowing it to occur.

I encourage you to be patient with yourself and to sit each day for a few silent moments. In addition, however, I urge you to make your daily life a meditation in motion. What I mean by this is reminding yourself to move about the tasks of your day with purpose, focus, and awareness. Enjoy one event, one experience, at a time.

For example, when you are taking your morning shower, be aware of the details of your experience; notice how the warm water feels pouring over your body and how the soap and shampoo smell. Appreciate each part of your body as you wash it, and pay attention to every detail. Don't think about that important meeting coming up at the office or the school lunches you need to fix. Those things will be attended to when the time comes, but for now, in this present moment, savor the luxurious experience of your shower, and enjoy every moment of it.

One reason we may feel discontent, become resentful, and neglect ourselves is because we miss the moments of wonder in our days. If our minds are constantly jumping back and forth from past to future and back to the past, the present eludes us, and we end up feeling short-changed. Our days pass by quickly, and if we never pause to extract the joy from the present moment, we are not really living. We are just moving forward hoping for peace, balance, and happiness, but we are forever waiting. We are then missing the joy and wonder contained in the present. We are missing the whole point!

Life is to be savored in the moment. (Sapphi knows this.) We need to think about things in order to be productive, but we need to balance "busy mind" times with quiet, reflective times. It is then that we make contact with our spirits and ourselves. In those quiet moments, our feelings deliver powerful, important messages to us, and we truly make connection with our authentic selves. Now back to little Sapphi.

When Sapphi is angry with me (for example, if I am a few minutes late attending to her needs, like throwing her ball, which she may perceive as an immediate need) and I ask her for a kiss, she turns her head to the side, raises her nose into the air, gazes at the ceiling, and refuses my request. This behavior lasts for five to ten seconds, and then I am showered with her wet, sloppy, loving kisses. She expresses her feelings, and then she lets her anger go. She doesn't spend the day harboring a grudge. Her feelings have been expressed and quickly dissipated. She doesn't mope about it or let resentment ruin an otherwise perfect day. She has moved on. We can benefit from this example.

Also, Sapphi doesn't worry about her weight. When the vet weighs her, she never frets because the numbers mean nothing to her. She is too busy watching the other people and animals in the waiting room. It is clear she is focused on the activity outside of herself. She knows she is perfect just as she is. She has the healthy attitude that we would all do well to adopt.

Animals do have much to teach. They model patience, tolerance, and unconditional love. Animals illustrate the importance of living in the moment and getting outside of ourselves. They promote health by making us laugh, and some take us for walks. Pets provide a source of comfort. They are faithful, nonjudgmental listeners. We can relate to our animal companions and benefit simply from having them in the room.

In addition to being my friend, Sapphi is also a registered therapy dog, and she spends many of her days working with me in my office. As I talk with clients, she sits nearby napping or chewing her bone. If asked, she will happily sit on a client's lap and accept attention. If clients cry or become upset, she will sit next to them and quietly comfort them. She lets them hug her when they need to and accepts their sobbing. She licks away their salty tears if they wish. She understands.

At other times, she will flip her bone into the air and chase it across the office floor. The session lightens, and clients focus outwardly for a minute. Her timing is perfect, and this break often helps clients to view their problems differently. A number have remarked that they enjoy seeing me, but it's really Sapphi whom they find most therapeutic. They laugh and then quickly follow this by saying they're joking, but I am sure there is an element of truth in what they say.

In 2006, my mother moved from Florida north to New Hampshire to be close to me. At the age of eight-six, she thought it was time to be near family who loved her and could help her. She had never been a "dog lover," but I must admit that once she met Sapphi, she seemed to prefer the company of my little dog to any human visitors. When I would call to see if it was a good time to stop by to say hello, her first question would be, "Do you have that fluffy little white dog with you?" If I answered yes, then I was assured permission to visit. Sapphi became my mother's therapist and wagged her tail with glee whenever I asked if she wanted to go to her Grammy's. My mother recently passed away at nearly ninety-two years young, but during her important final years, she and Sapphi had an extra special bond—a mutual connection of love. My mother lived a long and vibrant life, and I believe her healthy longevity was due, in large part, to her total enjoyment of Sapphi, her furry little pal.

If you do decide that having a pet may be helpful for you, then be thoughtful when selecting one. Not all animals are suitable for all situations. Talk with knowledgeable people about animals, and educate yourself before introducing a pet into your family. Some pets need space to run. Others are content to nap the day away in a small space. Some are friendly and affectionate, others aloof and independent. Do not rush into the pet shop and come home with a puppy or kitten simply because it is adorable and you have fallen in love with it. Find out as much as you can about it, and seriously consider whether or not it will be the perfect size and temperament for your situation. As animals are all different, so are we. So be sure you choose a pet that perfectly fits into your life situation and is compatible with your temperament.

Also, remember, there are wonderful, loving pets of all kinds waiting for adoption at animal shelters. These often make ideal choices. If you are unable to bring a pet into your home, you might volunteer to help at your local shelter. People are needed to brush or walk dogs, nurture and cuddle cats, and help in other ways with animals they have in residence. You will benefit greatly by feeling needed, getting exercise and companionship, and improving your self-esteem while you help the animals. It's a win-win situation!

So however you decide to rekindle your spiritual/creative connection, have fun. Stop being so serious! Let your passionate, free, fun-loving self emerge. Figure out what you need to do to bring more joy and zest into your life situation and then DO IT! This will make all the difference with your food-control issues. I promise!

PULL IT ALL TOGETHER

As we enter the final chapters of this book, I want to emphasize the importance of maintaining your sense of humor, exercising your mind, and seeing joy in all possible circumstances. In this busy world, it is all too easy to lose perspective. Instead of viewing our lives as a fantastic ride, we tend to focus on the speed bumps of unhappiness along the way.

We tend to see our lives as stagnant at times. We are here, these are our life circumstances, and that is our reality—frozen in time. We forget that life is ever changing and that all together it is just a blink of time. Tomorrows come quickly, and they come even more quickly as we age. If we don't make the changes we want to make now, then when? The future is always tomorrow, but then tomorrow becomes today and we still think we can make changes on another tomorrow. How many tomorrows do we expect to have?

Use what you read in this book to start right this minute. Today is your now. Seize this day and have as much fun as you can. Look for the joy in every circumstance. Use your mind and body to the fullest. And keep this in mind as you begin making healthy changes.

Below are a few things to consider before you craft your personal, flexible plan.

HAVE FUN

Many people who report they feel out of balance mentally, physically, and spiritually, seek my services as a psychologist. To soothe the painful feelings of depression, anxiety, and frustration, they often turn to overeating. They are wrapped up in the unhappiness that is part of life's experience, and they have forgotten the joy of being alive. Somewhere along the line, each of us forms our own idea of what it means to be an adult in today's world. Usually the definition is rigid and doesn't allow space for pleasure and fun. We become overly responsible, too serious, and fearful that we are not performing our adult roles well enough. In this section of the book, I encourage you to join with me in laughing at life and our own silly humanness.

Having fun and enjoying ourselves leads to balance and radiant health. How do you relax? What can you do to appreciate yourself and bring more joy into your life? The bottom line is that life is about feeling joyful. That is our purpose here, which sounds simple enough. But how exactly do we do this? Most of us haven't given this topic much, if any, thought. Since we have grown up and matured in a cultural climate that encourages us to work harder and faster and to submerge feelings of joy and fun, we may feel terribly guilty if we notice we are having fun and enjoying ourselves. Then we are likely to react by overeating to ease the discomfort of the guilt we feel for having fun and not attending to the serious demands of life.

We may also find ourselves working even harder and faster for many reasons—to gain social approval is a common one. Of course, the question is from whom do we imagine we need to get approval, and why do we think our worth is based on someone else's idea of whether or not we are living our lives in the "right" way? Have you ever thought about how ridiculous this is?

If you feel good, you know you are on the right path, a physically and emotionally healthy track. One way you know you are not choosing and doing what is best for yourself is if you don't feel good. Give some thought to where you find your happiness. Think about joyful experiences you have had in the past. Compile the longest list you can. Here are some of my personal favorites to get you started:

- Played with my dog

- Went bicycling for an hour at the shore

- Read a great novel and enjoyed every minute

- Experienced the fun of putting the last piece in a jigsaw puzzle

- Watched a great movie that made me laugh and cry

- Danced with wild abandon

Now add to your personal list and select one or two fun activities and make plans to do them. Then DO THEM!

As you have discovered by now, this book is not a diet book and is not about weight loss—not really. Your body, however, will shed pounds if that is what it wants to do to feel its best, especially when you begin to nurture yourself in other ways and give yourself what you truly want and need. The heart of the matter is you must figure out what you really need and give yourself that which you desire without feeling guilty if you are ever to achieve your goal of a vibrant, healthy body and a delicious life. You deserve no less than this.

EXERCISE YOUR MIND

You may not have thought much about the necessity of caring for your mind. All of the wonderful things you do for your body and your spirit will, of course, benefit your mind and help it to remain active and healthy. We cannot separate the mind from the entire being that we are. All our parts work together harmoniously to support each other. Your body tells your brain what it needs or wants, and your mind, through your thoughts, tells your body what it requires. Your spirit communicates with your mind and your body via your feelings. You now realize that all of this comprises your internal guidance system, which emits constructive messages being deciphered and sent to you by your partner, your well-trained Appetite. All this complex communication is taking place every moment. You are hardly aware of this endless conversation going on within your body, mind, and spirit. Together, though, you and your Appetite can figure out what the messages are that your feelings are trying to deliver to you.

One thing that we can do is supplement our diet with one teaspoon a day of the highest-quality fish oil. Your mind, which has always been sharp and quick, may no longer be quite as clear as it once was. Perhaps you have noticed that your mind occasionally goes blank while you are talking or you forget a word or two. This is a phenomenon I began to notice when I was approaching fifty. It was both frustrating and embarrassing. A few weeks of supplementing my diet with fish oil completely eliminated this problem. [2] You will be amazed at how much better your memory and concentration will be once you begin supplementing with this fabulous oil. We need to be conscious of our changing needs, especially as we age, and when taken regularly, fish oil not only helps brain cell integrity, it also helps lubricate our joints and enriches all of our organs and body system functions.

Drink an ample amount of pure water and choose the most nutritious, natural foods you can find. These will feed your brain as well. Remember, your brain also needs exercise. What do you do on a regular basis to challenge your mind? Puzzles, memory games, and anything that makes you think will be helpful. There are many books and games on the market today that can help with this.

CONSIDER SOCIAL FACTORS

You have received messages throughout your life about how you ought to look and not look, what you ought to do and not do, and what you ought to be thinking and feeling. These messages have had a great impact. Because of these, you have formed ideas about how you "should" lead your life. Your thoughts about how to live your life have been shaped by outside forces. This has resulted in faulty thinking. You have been trying to find happiness by doing what others think you *should* do or looking like what others think you *should* look like. If you have tried to be true to yourself and follow your own inner voice about how to look and what to do, chances are you have been greeted with disapproval at times. The pressure we each feel to conform is huge. To buck the system requires great courage and a fervent commitment to achieving your own well-being.

---

[2] Two excellent choices are fish oils from Carlson's and Nordic Naturals. You can locate these online, or ask your local health food store or holistic health practitioner to order them for you.

You have always been encouraged to diet and behave in ways that garner social approval. Friends, well-meaning family members, and the media all conspire in an attempt to make you feel inadequate. The majority of today's magazines, television shows, commercials, and infomercials (although some may be dispensing truly helpful advice) by and large deliver messages about ways to fix the flaws you obviously must have.

So here is the challenge. Think for yourself, and give up the notion of dieting. That's right. Tell yourself, "I will never diet again." Diets equal deprivation, and you have become convinced you must deprive yourself to bring your body down to a weight where you might find social approval. Chances are you have done this before, perhaps many times, and by now, you have figured out this not only doesn't work, but generally causes a weight gain that exceeds the weight where you started. You know in your core from years of repeating this frustrating, damaging cycle that diets do not work. So the next question is if diets don't work, what does?

What works is exactly the opposite of dieting—and I don't mean bingeing. Instead of depriving yourself, you must begin treating yourself as the goddess you are. Surround yourself with beauty, and fill your spaces at home and at work with things you love. At first, you may feel guilty, not imagining you deserve such royal treatment. Feelings of fear may creep in, and you might to want to eat junk food to ease the feelings that naturally accompany this kind of change. Remember, you are not being selfish. You are being self-loving, and that is the key to feeling well and letting go of self-destructive compulsive eating behaviors.

Your Appetite has now been trained to let you know through your uncomfortable feelings that you need to think about, and provide for yourself, what you truly need. The Appetite transmits this message to you through your feelings. Your job is to listen and work with your Appetite to provide yourself with whatever it takes for you to be happy. You know now it is not the junk food that gives you the true satiation you are seeking. It may be a nap or a hot bath or a brisk walk in the cool night air, but it is definitely not the empty calories you will find in chocolate bars, potato chips, and bowls of ice cream.

STEP V – Craft Your Personal Plan

Have you ever put a jigsaw puzzle together? Remember how gratifying it felt to put the final piece into place? Sorting out food-control issues and creating a life of balance, harmony, and joy is like putting a huge jigsaw puzzle together. Reading through the pages of this book has given you many puzzle pieces, and now it is time to put them all together so that your picture is clear.

Crafting your personal plan is the next step. It is an opportunity to pull together all you have learned from your reading. This plan will be flexible and serve as a map, guiding you from where you are to where you want to be.

First I will explain some of the voices we each have within us, urging us to sabotage ourselves and work against our own best interests. Then I will remind you of other voices that are there to help. At that point you will be ready to focus on what you need to do to take the very best care of yourself and create your delicious life and the body you have longed for.

You already know you must take care of yourself holistically—that is, from physical, emotional, social, spiritual, and environmental perspectives. If you look at food-control issues or other facets of your care from only one angle, you set yourself up to fail again and again. In this chapter you will find useful suggestions to implement a change from self-defeating behaviors to health-promoting ones. You will craft a personal self-care plan and then work with your now well-trained Appetite to implement this plan on a daily basis.

You understand how the food industry has manufactured and marketed foods to trick you into overeating. You know that diets cause weight gain. You are no longer going to fall into the binge/ diet trap as a way of caring for yourself. Now you are ready to focus on achieving radiant health, which can cause weight loss as a byproduct.

THE VOICES WITHIN

First, let's look at the many voices we all have in our heads—some urging us to overeat, some beating us up, and some putting us in the position of helpless victims. I will give a brief synopsis here. When I refer to the voices we hear, I am not saying we actually hear voices in our heads. These are voices that silently transmit messages. We are sending them to ourselves. These messages are thoughts based on old beliefs we have held for so long that they have become our truths.

The first one I will mention is the "saboteur" voice. This one says such things as, "Oh, you've really had a hard day, go ahead and treat yourself to some cookies," or "Sure you're angry. Go have a nice big bowl of ice cream. That will take the edge off those feelings." There is always a reason to eat, and you can rely on your saboteur to take every opportunity to remind you of how eating sugar, simple carbohydrates, salt and fat can help you feel better. The frustrating part is eating these dead foods does help, but only for a short while. In the long run, you end up feeling disappointed in yourself and even more frustrated.

Once you have listened to your saboteur and have eaten your fill, your next voice chimes in. This is the "critical parent" voice, and to shame you, it says, "You shouldn't have done that. What's the matter with you that you keep screwing up?" or "You should have gone for a walk. What a failure you are to sit there and eat all that!" The critical parent is the voice within each of us that reprimands us for not being perfect. It is the finger-pointing part of us that focuses on where we went wrong and how bad we are for not bypassing the cake in favor of a vegetable platter.

Once these two voices have spoken up and we have eaten the cookies and beaten ourselves to a pulp because of it, another familiar voice joins in. This is the "victim." This whining voice says things such as, "I can't help it. I try but fail every time. There is no hope. I am helpless to change. I will never be healthy and fit." This victim voice is natural for many of us because we have tried and failed repeatedly to get a handle on our out-of-control eating. Our cravings have been so strong at times, like the power of a wild horse's hooves stampeding across a field, that we have, indeed, felt helpless and just as out of control. The urges have seemed undeniable, and we have collapsed into food abuse as a way of stopping the chaos.

We soon feel badly about this behavior, however, and our saboteur is likely to chime in by saying, "Oh, you feel bad. You poor, helpless little thing! Have a big stack of pancakes with lots of butter and syrup, and you'll feel better." If you listen to your saboteur, the critical parent voice will follow close behind, and then you will hear your victim crying and whining louder than ever. This is a vicious cycle, and it is a cycle nearly everyone seems to identify with.

Think about your own experience. How often have you listened to your saboteur, who pretends to help you, only to fall victim to the self-deprecating messages of your internal critical parent? Have you beaten yourself up time and again for mindless overeating? I know I have spun in this way thousands of times, and it is a very difficult pattern to break. When you and your Appetite are working together, however, it becomes easier and you will be successful, not every single time, but more often than not.

You have another most important voice. This one will help you if you pay attention to it. This is what I call the "adult" voice. The adult voice is the voice of reason. It says such things as, "What are you really longing for right now? Will sugar really meet your needs in the long run?" Your adult voice begins each sentence with the words "Reality is…." Your loving adult says, "Reality is you did eat that cake. That's OK. Reality is you can now choose to do something different. Reality is that just because this time you gave in to that urge doesn't make you a bad person. Reality is through this experience you know more certainly what you don't want to do next time. Reality is it is a lesson, and you have paid attention to it. Now, let it go, move on, and enjoy the rest of your day." (You get the idea.)

Your old pattern of using food to take care of your unattended feelings doesn't really work for you anymore. You are too wise. You know this is not the way to happiness and health, and you now have a way to change this habitual, self-destructive behavior. Just as with a wild horse, you will have to be very tender, loving, and patient with yourself. If you beat your wild mustang, it will not be easy to train. In fact, it is highly unlikely to let you near it until a long period of trust-building takes place. And even then it may never let you train it successfully.

We are exactly the same. If we are harsh and critical of ourselves, if we beat ourselves up for following human instincts to dull or anni-hilate our feelings, we end up victims, and we perpetuate our cycle of self-abuse. Each time we scold or shame ourselves, we stay stuck in the overeating cycle.

You will be in charge when you have learned to take loving care of yourself instead of beating yourself up and to remain alert to the important messages your feelings are reliably transmitting via your Appetite. You will be able to step back and evaluate the situation and decide the very best course of action for yourself. You will be able to recognize your feelings and determine what you really need to feel truly satiated. It may be physical nourishment at times, but most likely, it will usually not be food-related.

Your adult voice works with another voice known as your "nurturing parent." This voice is loving and gentle. It soothes and calms you. You must learn ways to soothe yourself in the same ways as you would tend to a hurt child. Your nurturing parent may suggest a warm soak in the tub, a massage, or an evening out with friends. Your nurturing parent has your very best interests at heart, and in time, you will hear this voice more loudly and clearly.

By the way, the "brat" is another voice I will mention. We each have a brat inside who wants what we want, when we want it, and how we want it. Can you identify with this one? I can! The brat says, "I can have anything I want." This usually sends us back to the voices of the critical parent and victim once we have listened to it and fulfilled its demand for fudge or soda.

These voices are natural in all of us and are the best way for you to understand what has been going on with you for many years, perhaps a lifetime. Once you identify which voice is speaking to you through your thoughts, then you can decide what to do. You can jump into that self-defeating cycle once again or do something positive and different and attend to the feelings. You choose. It is your responsibility, and yours alone. Only you have the authority and the power to change yourself.

Also, I urge you to be aware that the feelings you are trying to deaden by eating are not always negative or painful at the start. We eat in this culture for an endless number of reasons. We eat to celebrate, and we eat when we are feeling fantastic and want to mark the good time with treats. Your saboteur is likely to say something like, "Hey! Isn't this a great party? It's so much fun. You can celebrate tonight with samplings of all those decadent desserts. Have a ball! How often can you find a spread like this one? And, while you're at it, have another few drinks. They're loaded with wonderful, soothing sugar. Go for it!"

Bear in mind that when you use alcohol, your inhibitions can easily be cast aside, and you are more likely to eat mindlessly, forgetting all of your healthy intentions. Drinking is risky. For many, it can represent a slippery slope, which one can easily slide down. Then you might find yourself once again entrenched in that old pattern of self-sabotage. So if you choose alcohol, be particularly aware that you are making yourself extra vulnerable. You may want to consider seltzer water and cranberry juice or some other nonalcoholic selection as an alternative.

Your good-feeling time can be ruined by your saboteur's voice. If you listen, throw caution to the wind, and dive head first into your dessert, you could end up in a negative cycle again. When your Appetite communicates with you, listen to it. It lets you know, through those urges to eat, that compulsive, emotional overeating is not really what is in your best interest. You will be happier, more relaxed, and better balanced once you learn the secret of attending to your feelings and giving yourself what you really need. You will not be able to do so every time but, as you practice working *with* your Appetite instead of *against* it, you will see remarkable differences in your attitude, your health, and eventually, in your bodily size.

When you heed the messages your Appetite delivers and want to make a choice other than stuffing yourself with nibbles, it is important that you have a plan. Alternatives to overeating must be readily at hand. If you don't have a plan, you are likely to repeat the same old behaviors, and you know where those are likely to lead. Before we craft a plan, I want to repeat some of what you already know for emphasis.

You have learned to care for yourself in many ways—to feed your mind and body and to nourish your spirit. You have thought of ways to care for your body. For example, you recognize your need for nourishing food, sunshine, good-quality sleep, suitable shelter, and clothing. You know you need to move about, stretch, and exercise your muscles regularly, and you are aware of the vital importance of drinking enough pure water to stay hydrated.

You are learning to access, name, and express your feelings and are becoming more emotionally healthy. You realize the importance of asserting yourself at times and communicating clearly and directly. Once your Appetite has alerted you to incoming feeling messages, you know it is important for you to attend to them. You also know that based on what these messages are telling you, you will have many possible actions you can take to meet your real needs.

You know ways to nurture and care for your spirit. You recognize the importance of solitude and reflection. You know it is necessary to play, laugh, and relax. You are aware that your mischievous, artistic, courageous, playful, loving, and curious parts represent your spiritual energies. They are your passion and beauty. You are now ready to craft and implement the perfect plan for you!

CREATE YOUR PERSONAL PLAN

You can create your own personal, flexible plan for permanently changing self-destructive overeating behavior. Your plan will be specific to you and contain only steps that you are comfortable taking to correct the physical, emotional, social, environmental, and spiritual imbalances that have led you to disregard your true needs in the past. Drafting this plan provides you with the map you need to follow on your road to recovery. This self-care plan serves as an indispensable tool you can use daily to assure radiant health, well-being and your delicious life.

To make your personal plan, consider things you would like to do for yourself on physical, emotional, social, spiritual, and environmental levels. To assure success, you need to look holistically at the full picture. At first, this may seem daunting, but it is doable and well worth putting effort into. Within your plan, you will be looking at each smaller part, and at the end, you will have a long list of things to choose from to take care of yourself in a loving way.

Take a journal or a pad of paper or open your word processing program and title each page with one of the following: General Suggestions, Physical, Emotional, Social, Spiritual, and Environmental.

You are now ready to brainstorm those things in each category which you know will be helpful to you every day, especially when your Appetite has sent you messages to attend to and you have chosen not to follow your knee-jerk overeating reaction. I will give you some suggestions that you can feel free to use. Eliminate anything that does not appeal to you, and add things you prefer that I haven't thought of. Remember, this is for you. You are making a list of suggestions in each category to turn to on a daily basis that will help you make the most intentional, self-loving choices possible. For example, when you are feeling self-destructive urges, reviewing your lists will generate awareness and help you get back into balance.

On your first page titled "General Suggestions," you can list things you might enjoy doing instead of abusing yourself by overeating. This page is meant to give you quick ideas to help you get back on track when your intentions have fallen by the wayside. The following are lists of examples for each one of your pages:

General Suggestions
- Sit quietly for a few minutes.

- Do some yoga postures.

- Play inspiring, classical, or relaxing music.

- Dance to an upbeat tune.

- Get a massage.

- Relax in a hot bubble bath.

- Do some type of aerobic activity.

- Light some candles, burn incense, and use fragrant lotions or essential oils for a dose of aromatherapy.

- Put my feet up and read a good book.

- Watch a funny movie and laugh.

- Call a supportive friend and chat.

- Get outside and take a long walk.

- Utilize one way I know to lower my stress level right now.

Physical

- Reduce or eliminate caffeine from my diet.

- Detoxify from sugar and simple carbohydrates.

- Take suitable vitamin supplements and fish oil.

- Increase my water consumption to at least sixty-four ounces per day to remain hydrated.

- Exercise at least three times a week, even if it is just for a short time.

- Get plenty of rest and good-quality sleep.

- Get out in the sun for at least a few minutes every day.

- Breathe deeply out in the fresh air.

- Exercise my mind with challenging mental activities.

Emotional

- Identify my emotions. Write down what I am feeling right now.

- Think of what I truly need to do to take care of these feelings.

- Communicate my feelings to a supportive person or an appropriate helper.

- Check in with my support system and let them know that I need their support right now.

- Soothe my feelings without food. Take a nap, read for a few minutes, or take a bath.

- Write my feelings down in my journal.

- Make a list of things I am grateful for. Start a gratitude journal.

Social

- Attend to my relationships. Whom haven't I touched base with lately? Give them a call or send an e-mail.

- Remind myself to disregard those harmful socialization messages I received about behaving perfectly or being the perfect weight. Those messages were wrong!

- Tune in to my comfort level. Do I need some social time right now, or do I need solitude? What do I really want?

- Do I need to give myself an attitude adjustment? Shall I shower myself with positive messages instead of bombarding myself with negative ones?

Spiritual

- Give myself quiet time to reflect on where I am right now with these feelings.

- Do something creative, like draw, paint, or model with clay.

- Be playful and have fun. Arrange a play date for myself, alone or with a friend, to do something I love.

- Pray.

- Do some spiritual reading.

- Meditate.

- Remind myself to be mindful.

- Play joyful or soothing music, depending on my mood.

Environmental
- Create the environment of my dreams.

- Decorate with colors and textures that please me.

- Make a space with as much sunshine flooding into it as possible.

- Throw away things I no longer need or want.

- Make my space a haven—as neat and orderly as I would like it to be.

(Do not try to feel energetic in a disorganized, cluttered place. Remember, such an environment will drain your Chi, or energy.)

Now let me give you a few examples of how you can use the pages you have created to your best advantage. One way is to first turn to the general suggestions page. Here you will find the list you have made of activities to do instead of eating when you want to eat and you know it is not physical hunger you are experiencing. You may also browse through your pages and think about things you really need, like a nap, some sunshine, or a big drink of water. As you read some of your own ideas, chances are you will become aware of areas in your life that need attention. Perhaps you will want to sort out those old clothes and donate a bag to charity or pick up litter in your yard.

What you have created serves not only to give you suggestions for things to do right away to avoid overeating, but also gives you much to think about and check in with yourself about your daily self-care. Add new ideas to your pages that you discover over time, and likewise, eliminate from them anything that is no longer helpful. Keep your pages handy for reference every single day as you renew your commitment to yourself and your best care. Reading them over will help you stay in touch with your desire and commitment to be the healthiest, happiest, most positive person you can be.

It is easy to forget about ourselves and ignore our own needs. Keep your plan handy, and review it regularly (as often as possible). This practice helps you keep your good intentions alive. Each item on your list serves as a reminder that you are worth caring about. At first, I suggest you make a copy of your plan to carry with you to read and reread whenever you can. Doing so will help you permanently change your automatic response of grabbing food to fill your needs.

The crafting of your plan offers many suggestions of things you can do or write about. Remember, it behooves you to pick up your pages each day and spend about twenty minutes every morning just planning your day ahead. These pages contain so many ideas to choose from! If you give thought in advance to how you wish to proceed through the day, you are likely to have a day that is positive. You are actively choosing your experience instead of passively reacting to whatever happens to come along. If you just thoughtlessly leap out of bed at the last minute and charge out the door, you are more likely to fall prey to those urges to handle things by choosing unhealthy snacks and overeating. Need I remind you that positive attracts more positive just as negative pulls more negative aspects into your experience?

SUMMARY

To be your naturally healthy, vibrant, beautiful self and to radiate positive energy at whatever weight your body feels best, you must consider your total well-being. It is no longer possible for you to think in terms of calories in, calories out as your guide. It is more complicated than that, yet it is paradoxically simple as well.

When you focus on what you do not like, you attract more of what you don't like. the Law of Attraction assures that. If you think self-destructive thoughts such as, "I really am fat, and I need to lose these ugly pounds," you will feel badly, and in so doing, you will attract more "bad-feeling" thoughts. You will get stuck in a loop of negative thinking, which leads to negative behaviors, extra pounds, increased worries, stronger efforts to diet, more deprivation, discouragement, guilt, shame, and fear of gaining more and more weight.

This can lead to depression, increased anxiety, and eventual apathy. You are then likely to submerge yourself in sugar, simple carbohydrates, salt and fat to anesthetize yourself for the few moments, hours, or days of relief that you know these substances can and reliably will provide.

Once done with this cycle, you regroup and plan your next strategy for losing those pounds that you are sick and tired of hauling around. Perhaps this time a new diet has captured your attention or you saw a new exercise machine advertised that is guaranteed to melt your pounds away effortlessly and at warp speed. You enthusiastically embrace your new course of action. You are hopeful and optimistic. You pray that this time you have hit upon exactly the right method to achieve the weight loss you have searched for so desperately.

Your newly designed plan may work for a while, but unless you accompany your efforts with lifestyle modifications, you are likely to find your well-intentioned self stuck in the same habits you so recently broke. You are likely to feel more frustrated, discouraged, and depressed than before. It is of great value to learn to feed and care for your whole self properly.

You are wise to the scams of the food industry. You have learned the difference between normal and emotional eating and are making friends with yourself more and more every day. You are now aware of how you could be setting yourself up to fail by expecting yourself to behave perfectly at all times. By now, you can see that this has not gotten you where you want to go. These impossible, self-imposed ideals of appearance and behavior have kept you from relaxing and enjoying your life. You have been trying too hard to accomplish your impossible goals. It is time now to stop, relax, and really give yourself what you truly want.

STEP VI – Honor Yourself

If you want to succeed in your efforts to take the best care of yourself possible, you must first make a sincere commitment to honor yourself—your body and your soul. If you read this book and then set it aside or give it away, you will most likely revert back to the self-defeating, frustrating feelings that caused you to pick it up in the first place. Honoring yourself—and reminding yourself every day to do so—is crucial. I suggest you write a contract stating that you will honor yourself, your feelings, and your needs at all times. Then sign this agreement and carry it with you or post it as a reminder to renew your contract with yourself every single day.

Here is a sample contract you can use. Or write one yourself that includes the specific ways you want to help yourself along your path to radiant health and happiness.

CONTRACT

I _____

hereby promise to make myself and my care number one on my list of priorities from this day forward. I will pay attention to the messages my feelings transmit to me and make my best effort to listen to and heed the valuable information I am receiving. I will do my best to eat well, stay hydrated, exercise, have fun, get plenty of rest, and nurture my relationships. I will give myself quiet time every day to connect with my inner spirit.

I release my perfectionistic self-expectations and embrace my humanness. I know I am perfect just as I am. I am lovable, and I will honor myself as such. I accept myself fully, and I realize there are no mistakes, only lessons.

Signed _____

Date _____

Becoming friendly with yourself helps. Once you accept who you are and become gentle and nonjudgmental with yourself, you make swift progress toward the ideal body size, vibrant health, and balance you want so badly. You have been offered many suggestions within these pages, and it is up to you to choose which seem best for you. Your personal plan provides a map for you to follow, but you must figure out precisely your own direction and destination.

You now know about the Law of Attraction and the premise that like attracts like. It is up to you to pay attention to any and all negative thoughts you harbor about yourself and your body. Each time you recognize that you are beating yourself up with these unhealthy thoughts, pause, breathe, and substitute a positive thought. Gradually, you will find that your thoughts have shifted to positive ones, and your life will become more positive in the process.

As you courageously shift your perspective in this way, you move quickly toward your delicious life of radiant health and balance. You now recognize the importance of paying attention to your thoughts and feelings and know these feelings represent your internal guidance system, which is *never* wrong. Now you know where to turn to decide what to do every minute—inside yourself rather than outside. Your internal guidance system will never steer you in the wrong direction. If you make yourself number one and heed the messages your feelings are delivering through this system as consistently as possible, you will move closer and closer to your goals.

Remember, this is *your* life and *your* body to do with as you wish. It doesn't matter what anyone else is doing, thinking, or telling you. Keeping yourself murky and drugged with unhealthy foods will never bring you the happiness you deserve. To be healthy, whole, and joyful is the goal. If it is to be, it is up to you, and the time is NOW!

My very warmest wishes for continued success on your special journey.

Many Blessings!
Dr. Denise

Critical Concepts

In this final chapter I summarize the most salient points from each section to help you recall and refresh the teachings of the entire book. As you read through them, highlight the ones that are particularly important for you. By revisiting this final section from time to time, you will keep what you have learned alive and reinforce your efforts to take the best loving care of yourself.

Diets DO NOT work! They actually cause weight gain. Depriving yourself will lead to overeating. Starving always leads to stuffing.

Diets foster a lifestyle of deprivation, and if you severely restrict your caloric intake and deny yourself the pleasure of savoring foods you love, you will build resentment. You will also lower your metabolism, which makes weight loss or weight management more difficult.

Remember that the food industry conspires against us by adding addictive properties (sugar, simple carbohydrates, salt and fat) to many foods we eat and by advertising products as healthy when, in fact, many are not. It is easy to keep eating far beyond our satiation points. Share your meal with a friend or box half to take home before you begin eating. Be vigilant about portion sizes.

The intention is not to diet, but to strive for balance. Strive for balance physically, emotionally, socially, and spiritually. You deserve nothing less!

Seeking instant gratification leads to overeating, followed by punishing periods of deprivation—starving yourself alternating with stuffing your body until you fall upon your bed at night like a beached whale. Learn and practice other ways to soothe yourself while waiting for the urge to eat immediately to subside. Then you will be able to make intelligent, self-loving choices (most of the time).

The goal is to feel good about yourself as you use your intuitive guidance system to set your own standards for your health and well-being. The mandates of our society to be thin are damaging. Determine what body size is right for you. Decide what the healthiest lifestyle is for you personally. *Only* you can do this.

Most people, mainly women, are confused and hold fast to the perfectionistic self-expectations that have led them to fail again and again. You can strive for perfection but you will inevitably wind up feeling like a failure if you hold perfection as a goal you "should" or "must" attain. Common sense tells you that trying to be perfect in every way is an impossible goal. If you set this standard for yourself, you will fail—every time. Instead, set realistic goals that are challenging, but not impossible. Review your goals from time to time to see if they are still relevant, worthy, and possible.

There is no simple answer. Food-control issues are about more than simply calories in, calories out. Creating peace, balance, and ideal weight requires that you address your entire being—your physical, emotional, social, spiritual and environmental needs. Take out your personal plan every day and review it to remind yourself of the importance of addressing all of your needs. This regular review is necessary to keep your healthy intentions and total care in focus.

The reality is you do know what to do. The answers lie deep within you, but the barrage of messages you receive from the outside world is confusing. You can find your own answers and empower yourself to act in your own best interests.

Remind yourself again and again that <u>you are perfect just as you are</u>. You will not, however, ever be able to behave "perfectly" in every instance. Print this message on index cards and put them everywhere—on your bureau, in your car, on your desk, etc. The more you read this message, the more it will be registered in your brain, and the more liberated and empowered you will feel.

No lifetime can ever conform to your image of unrealistic perfection. You must accept this. Realizing your limitations is difficult, but freeing. This is a core issue for many of us. Letting go of the pressure to be perfect changes your perspective and enables you to allow yourself to be human. Then you can accept yourself and stop beating yourself up when you inevitably make human errors. You can simply smile at yourself, recognize your humanness, and move on. In doing so, you free yourself of the urge to berate yourself and are no longer stuck with your frustration and guilty feelings.

Make yourself number one on your list of people to care for. It only makes sense that you do so. The better you attend to yourself, the better you will feel. As difficult as it may sound, you have to take the very best care of yourself. If you don't, who will? It is your job, and your life will be delicious, joyful, and free of overeating when your real needs are satisfied.

If you are living your life in service of everyone else and neglecting yourself, you are telling yourself that you do not deserve to be treated as well as others. You are telling yourself that you are not important, while somewhere deep inside, you know that you are!

Being self-loving means attending to your own needs and making yourself as important—not less or more—as everyone else. Give yourself the best of care. Treat yourself well, and lavish yourself with attention.

Many women think that being self-loving means being selfish. This is faulty thinking. Being selfish does not feel good. Being self-loving does. Feeling good is the most important thing for you to strive for. Recall that feeling good leads to more good feelings, more positive experiences, and more energy.

"Like attracts like unto itself" therefore, the more positive thoughts you have, the more positive you feel, and the more positive experiences and feelings you will attract. Practice reaching for better-feeling thoughts. The better you feel, the better you will feel.

When you befriend your Appetite and pay close attention to the valuable communication it brings, you begin to value it as a true friend instead of a foe. Practice deciphering the messages your Appetite is delivering. Once you are able to do that, you will be well equipped to make more self-loving choices.

To craft your ideal life, you must be clear about what your desires actually are and learn to be positive as much as possible. When you are making choices that are in your best interest, you will discover that overeating is no longer a viable option.

Your feelings constantly and faithfully deliver messages from your internal guidance system via your Appetite about what choices are in your best interest in all aspects of your life. Think of this in terms of all situations. Your feelings always tell you what you need to do to stay on your path regarding eating, communicating with others, behaving in social situations, etc.

It is a beautiful thing when you balance your need to attend to yourself with attending to others' needs. It is when you allow others' needs to crowd yours out of the picture that a problem arises. Think of yourself holding a scale of justice. In your mind, visualize your needs on one side of the scale and others' needs on the other side. If your side of the scale is way up high and the other side is weighted down, then that is a sure sign that you have been neglecting yourself. Do something to change that balance right now!

Again, your persistent feelings make up your internal guidance system and, as such, are constantly providing the information you require to make the very best choices for yourself in each moment. Following your intuition means paying close attention to these feelings and heeding the messages they are transmitting. To take full advantage of these important communications, you must pay attention to what you are feeling and heed the instructions you are being given. It is helpful to write down feelings that repeatedly come to the surface for you and then figure out what you must do for yourself to feel better. I have repeated this now a number of times for emphasis. It is the central concept of this book.

Finding happiness is your life's purpose and your most important task. Life ought to be fun. Do all you can to make it that way. Think about things you enjoy and then do them. Don't allow the seriousness of daily living to crowd out the wonder of the moment.

We are humans who spend much time doing and not much time being. Why not slow down, relax, and focus for a while on what *you* truly want? Why not do this several times a day? It will become a habit that will serve you well. Most people go through the routine of their day with the goal of making it to the evening and then the next day. If you robotically move through your days, weeks, months, and years on autopilot, you are not likely to experience much variety and joy. It is your job to create a full and happy life, but you can only do so if you stop and pay attention to your desires.

A morning routine of meditation, journaling, or any form of introspection will help you do this. It will take patience and practice. Isn't it amazing how swiftly the days pass? Make each one of your days count!

It is vital to assert yourself and communicate what your wants and needs truly are. You deserve to ask for what you want and express yourself. Your feelings are no more or less important than anyone else's. You may not always get what you ask for, but often you will. Then, even when you don't get what you asked for, you'll feel better knowing you expressed yourself instead of stifling your thoughts and feelings and building resentments.

Speaking up and standing up for yourself will empower you, and you will not need food as medication. It is when you hold your thoughts and feeling inside and they remain unexpressed that you are likely to rebel or punish yourself for your silence by overeating. This may be difficult at first because you may fear others won't like you if you express yourself. Most people who truly care about you will be eager to hear how you feel. If they don't care, then ask yourself why you want them in your life at all.

When you move through your feelings and experience them instead of avoiding them, you end up in a much more calm and peaceful place. You are then working as a team with your Appetite to make decisions based on your true desires. This will feel natural after a while, and you are likely to notice less anxiety, less depression, less frustration, and more peace and joy.

Movement through the stages of your life will inevitably stir emotions deep within, whether you are conscious of them at the time or not. Each progression through the years brings adjustments with it. As you let a time in your life go, you anticipate your emergence into a new time. It is natural to experience anxiety through these transitions. You can develop ways to calm your anxiety and soothe yourself without giving in to your familiar pattern of using sugar, simple carbohydrates, salt and fat.

It is essential that you do not let the opinions and feelings of others deter you from following your dreams. After all, this is your life, and it is your responsibility to make of it what you want. Other people may want you to follow a path they have decided is best for you. Don't do it! Follow your heart. Your internal guidance system will never steer you in the wrong direction.

Remaining fixated on the past and being a perpetual victim will keep you in a state of anxiety and reactivity, and you will never take action to make the adjustments necessary to craft your life as richer and more rewarding. When you find yourself ruminating about how things were in your past, redirect your thought to the present time. You can't ever change the past. You know this, but those old thoughts and feelings are hard to let go of. This is a great time to recite affirmations ("I am fine right this minute.") and appreciations ("I am blessed to have such a strong and healthy body.") or to meditate, pick up your journal, get some exercise, or call a friend for support.

Your path requires you to greet the circumstances of each moment with awareness and to experience each and every feeling that passes through your body. It may sound easy, but it is not. It takes practice to experience your feelings and move on. It is possible, however, and the most important work you can do. Accept that there are twists and turns along your own path of life. Experience every valuable feeling. Give yourself what you need in the moment, and your life will change in positive ways.

When you feel butterflies in your stomach, observe this sensation. That is only your anxiety. Underlying this is always a fear that you are not lovable. YOU ARE. You can trust this! So pay attention to the messages the butterflies are delivering, and do something loving for yourself. Others may treat you lovingly from time to time, but you cannot count on them to "make" you feel worthy. This is a job that you alone can do, and you must do it!

Remember, it is never too late to try something new. You are never too old to have fun! Separate yourself from all the roles you play in life—parent, child, friend, partner, etc.—and spend time thinking of who you are and what you would like to do for fun. Be creative and find ways to be playful and joyous—alone or with others.

Spend time contemplating what you love to do. You cannot create something new in your life if you don't spend time thinking about what you want. Devote time to discovering who you are. Only then can you move toward the life you truly want to have—filled with zest, joy, health, and balance. Notice what you like and what does not please you. Then follow the positive feelings and you will be on the very best path!

To stop any compulsive behavior, to heal your body, you must attend to your spirit and treat yourself with patience, compassion, and love. Many of us know this on a deep and private level. Life has brought you varied experiences. Some have most likely been positive, others not. You have been treated well at times and poorly at others. The result is the injuries of your past have left open wounds, and chances are your spirit has been hurt. Now is the time to tend to those old wounds and heal your spirit. Then will you will begin to value and nurture your body.

Self-loving choices are spiritually enhancing, and the more you make, the better you will feel, and the less compulsive, self-harming choices you will make. When you make a less than self-loving choice (and you will because we all do at times), observe yourself. Notice how you feel physically, emotionally, and spiritually. Without judging, just notice how you feel when you are harming yourself. This awareness will help you be more self-loving in the future.

Your choices to eat foods that you instinctively know are not good for your health or your decision to overeat at times are not mistakes. There are no mistakes, only lessons. Again, just notice how you feel when you do step off your path and that knowledge will help you make better choices in the future. Do not dwell on what you have done and beat yourself up. Be grateful for the lesson and move on.

Practice making self-loving choices. When you do make a self-loving choice, you are likely to feel proud of yourself. You will have more physical energy and will feel more lovable and more connected to yourself, your family, others, and the world in general. The more you stop and consider your alternatives and make your choices in the spirit of love, the more you will notice that peace, lightness, and joy manifest in your life.

What you think about is what you draw into your life, and the Law of Attraction is as real and reliable as the Law of Gravity. So when you give thought to something, you invite it into your life. Weight loss and management can really be as simple as changing your thought patterns. This is difficult to imagine, but it really can. In fact, weight loss is impossible without shifting your thoughts to a positive vibration whenever possible.

If you persist in saying "I am fat," for example, the Universal Law of Attraction assures you that you will remain in a state of feeling and being fat. If instead you focus on the fabulous things about your body and you visualize yourself as healthy and slender, you raise your vibrational, positive energy and move steadily closer to realizing that vision of yourself.

You can do and have and be anything you want. You create this through your thoughts, visions, words, and feelings. You are the changer and the changed, and you always get what you think about. So pay attention to your thoughts and the feelings that come as a result. As you pay close attention to these feelings, you will be better equipped to change your thoughts, which will, in turn, enable you to change your feelings and create precisely what you need at any time.

The sugar, simple carbohydrates, salt and fat you are reaching for will only make you feel better momentarily. In a short while, you are likely to feel fat, guilty, and ashamed and crave more treats, which will only serve to continue the discouraging, frustrating cycle of feeling bad, eating more, feeling worse, eating more, gaining weight, feeling discouraged, eating more, and so on. This cycle leads to increased anxiety, depression, and weight gain.

Take advantage of Bach® Flower Remedies. If you are in crisis or just having a difficult time, the Bach® Flower blend known as Rescue Remedy can help you through.

The Bach® blend known as Rescue Sleep can help you if you have trouble either falling asleep or returning to a sleep state after awakening during the night. Rescue sleep quiets your mind so your body can get the proper rest so essential to your well-being. Remember, if you do not get sufficient, good-quality sleep, your body produces more of the hormones that increase Appetite (ghrelen and cortisol) and fails to produce the satiation hormone (leptin).

There are a few tinctures that have been found to be effective in helping with emotional overeating problems. These are Chestnut Bud (which helps you learn from your mistakes), Cherry Plum (which helps you stay in control), and Crabapple (which helps you appreciate and befriend your body). These are available individually or in the Bach® Emotional Eating Support Kit.

However you decide to rekindle your spiritual/creative connection, have fun. Stop being so serious! Forget negative remarks anyone ever made to stifle your spirit. They didn't know what they were talking about! Let your passionate, free, fun-loving self emerge. Figure out what you need to do to bring more joy and zest into your situation and then DO IT! You are creating your delicious life.

Maintain your sense of humor, exercise your mind, and see joy in all possible circumstances. In this busy world, it is all too easy to lose perspective. Make time for your passion. Don't delay your fun. Tomorrows come quickly, and they come even more quickly as you age. If you don't make the changes you want to make now, then when will you?

Having fun and enjoying yourself leads to balance and radiant health. A delicious life is a joyful one. Creating that is your purpose here! If you feel good, you know you are on the right path, a physically and emotionally healthy track. If you do not feel good, then you are not choosing and doing what is best for you. You have strayed from your path.

Your body will shed pounds if that is what it wants to do to feel its best, especially when you begin to nurture yourself in other ways and give yourself what you truly want and need. You must figure out what you really need and give yourself that which you desire without feeling guilty. You deserve no less than this.

Remain conscious of your changing needs, especially as you age. When taken regularly, fish oil can help. It not only helps brain cell integrity, but it also helps lubricate your joints and enriches all of your organs and body system functions.

Ask your health care professional to test your Vitamin D level. This vitamin, which is essential for energy and vitality, is obtained via sunshine and most of us (nearly all of us who live in climates where we have little sunshine during parts of the year) are deficient in this vital nutrient. The major function of vitamin D is maintaining normal blood levels of calcium and phosphorus. It helps with the formation and maintenance of strong bones and may provide protection from osteoporosis and hypertension (high blood pressure). It helps with maintaining the nervous system, regulating heart function, normalizing blood clotting and a number of autoimmune diseases. It is also thought to play a role in cancer prevention as well as in multiple sclerosis and type 2 diabetes treatments.

Drink an ample amount of pure water and choose the most nutritious, natural foods you can find. These will feed your brain as well. And, remember, your brain also needs exercise and rest. As any living creature needs to be nurtured, so do you—in every aspect of your self-care.

Your thoughts about how to live your life have been shaped by outside forces. This has resulted in faulty thinking. You have been trying to find happiness by doing what others think you *should* do or by trying to look like what others think you *should* look like. Forget them. This is your body, your life, and every single choice is yours, and yours alone.

Begin thinking for yourself, and give up the notion of dieting. That's right. Tell yourself, "I will never diet again." Diets equal deprivation, and you have become convinced you must deprive yourself to bring your body down to a weight where you might find social approval. This will NEVER work! Not only does dieting not work, it generally causes a weight gain that exceeds the weight where you started. If you are like me, you know this in your core from years of repeating this frustrating, damaging, yo-yo cycle.

Instead of depriving yourself, treat yourself as the god or goddess you are. Surround yourself with beauty, and fill your spaces at home and at work with things you love. Create a sanctuary in your home. Add music, candles, flowers, or anything that brings you peaceful, joyous feelings. You are not being selfish. You are being self-loving, and that is the key to feeling good and letting go of self-destructive compulsive eating behaviors.

Your Appetite transmits messages to you through your feelings. Your job is to listen and work with your Appetite to provide yourself with whatever it takes to be happy. This means taking care of yourself holistically—that is, from physical, emotional, social, spiritual, and environmental perspectives. If you look at food-control issues or other facets of your care from only one angle, you set yourself up to fail again and again.

Remind yourself that eating sugar, simple carbohydrates, salt and fat can only help you feel better for a little while. This behavior never helps for long, and you will end up feeling disappointed in yourself and even more frustrated.

You are most likely beating yourself up for following your human instincts to dull or annihilate your feelings. If you continue to do this, you will end up feeling like a victim and perpetuate your cycle of self-abuse. Each time you scold or shame yourself, you assure that you will remain stuck in the overeating cycle. You will be in charge when you have learned not to beat yourself up and to remain alert to the important messages your feelings are reliably transmitting.

As you become more skilled at recognizing your feelings and determining what you really need to feel truly satiated, you empower yourself to provide what you really need for your happiness. It may be physical nourishment at times, but most likely, it will usually not be food-related.

Search for ways to soothe yourself just as you would nurture a hurt child. Your nurturing parent may suggest a warm soak in the tub, a massage, or an evening out with friends. Your needs are individual, and what may be soothing for someone else may not work for you. Think of options that please you, and begin lavishing yourself with love and attention.

It is important that you have a plan. Alternatives to overeating must be readily at hand. If you don't have a plan, you are likely to repeat the same old behaviors, and you know where those can lead. Review the holistic plan that you created at least once a day. Change it as your needs change. This will help you stay focused on your commitment to yourself and your movement toward permanent change.

Your personal plan contains so many creative ideas to choose from! Each morning, read the plan that you crafted and spend about twenty minutes planning your day. If you give thought in advance to how you wish to proceed, you are likely to have a day that is positive. If you get up and approach your day without conscious consideration, you are likely to do exactly what you have always done in the past. Your goal is to behave differently and make self-loving choices as often as possible.

It is necessary to access, name, and express your feelings to be emotionally healthy. People around you are not mind readers, and they are not likely to know how you feel if you don't tell them. They may not appreciate it when you begin expressing yourself, but in the long term, this will help any worthwhile relationship you have to flourish. It is holding feelings in and stuffing them down with food that erodes relationships.

You know ways to nurture and care for your spirit. You recognize the importance of solitude and reflection. You know it is necessary to play, laugh, and relax. You are aware that your mischievous, artistic, courageous, playful, loving, and curious parts represent your spiritual energies. They are your passion and beauty. You also know that to live the fullest, most wonderful, delicious life possible you must express yourself.

You made your personal plan, and you considered things you would like to do for yourself on physical, emotional, social, spiritual, and environmental levels. Now make your plan work for you. This bears repeating. I urge you to review your plan on a daily basis. This will help you make the most intentional, self-loving choices possible. Without doing so, it is all too easy to fall back into old, frustrating, self-destructive behaviors.

Do not try to feel energetic in a disorganized, cluttered place. Such an environment will drain your Chi, or energy. Look around the rooms in your living and working spaces as well as your car. What can you throw away, give away, or sell? How can you clear the clutter and make the space that will bring you peaceful feelings? If you have difficulty with this, you can invite a friend over to help. Make it fun, and when you are done, make a cup of tea and sit and experience the peace that comes with an energy-filled, spacious environment.

By making yourself number one and connecting with your Appetite, you create your delicious life and the body you long for!

Dr. Denise's Programs and Services include:

Keynotes
Workshops
Individual therapy
Group therapy
Private Telephone Consultations
Teleseminars
Wellness & Holistic Health Programs

Contact her office for information about her speaking services and workshops, class registrations or appointments at:
603-493-6043, denise@deniselamothe.com

Stay Connected To Dr. Denise:

Sign-up for Dr. Denise's helpful free newsletter, *The Chew Tamer's Journey*, at www.deniselamothe.com.

While you are visiting www.deniselamothe.com, stop in at Dr. Denise's store for helpful books, CDs and other products to assist you on your journey.

Find weekly postings at www.chewtamers.blogspot.com.

Join Dr. Denise on Facebook, http://www.Facebook.com/DrDeniseLamothe.

Thank you for reading this book! Dr. Denise loves to hear from her readers and looks forward to learning about your exciting progress! *Keep in touch!*

denise@deniselamothe.com

www.deniselamothe.com
www.drdenise.org
www.chewtamers.blogspot.com
www.theappetiteconnection.com
www.emotionalovereatingawareness.com
www.jigsawconsulting.org